Victoriously

He

Makes All Things

New

# Victoriously He Makes All Things New

### Kim D. Sharpton

ANOINTED ROSE PRESS™

ANOINTED ROSE PRESS™

The Anointed Rose Press name and logo are registered Trademarks
of ANOINTED ROSE PRESS™ PUBLISHING

# Victoriously He Makes All Things New©

### KIM SHARPTON
Email: kim.sharpton15@gmail.com

ISBN-13: 978-0-9896110-3-9
ISBN-10: 0-9896110-3-5
©2017 by Kim Sharpton

Anointed Rose Press
Upper Darby, PA 19082
Email: anointed.rose.press@gmail.com

---

Library of Congress Control Number: 2017950818
Library of Congress Catalog-in-Publication Data

Sharpton, Kim

Victoriously He Makes All Things New / Kim Sharpton
p.cm.

ISBN (trade pbk.: alk. Paper)

11  12 13 14 15 16 17        AnR LS        1 2 3 4 5 6 7 8 9 10

1.Religion:Christian Life-Women's Issues  2. Family & Relationships: General

**Cover Design/Editor:**
ANOINTED ROSE PRESS/September Summer
Upper Darby, PA (484) 378-0939

*Printed in the USA for worldwide distribution. May not be reproduced or transmitted for commercial purposes, except for brief quotations in printing, without permission from the publisher*

DEDICATION PAGE

I dedicate *"Victoriously He Makes All Things New"* to my children Delecia, Michael and Nichelle; to my ten grandchildren John, Israel, Delecia, Aiyanna, Jasmine, Kaelyn, Jaeson, Austin and Ryan; to my mother Mary Sharpton; to my spiritual mother Romelle Ward-Adams; and to all who are victorious and know that Jesus is responsible for making all things New.

# EPIGRAPH

As I picked the landscape of the mountains this song rung in my spirit:

Kurt Carr – *"For every mountain You brought me over*
*For every trial you've seen me through*
*For every blessing, Hallelujah*
*For this I give You praise"*

God has brought me through many hurdles, obstacles, pains, hurts, trials, and tests. Those are the mountains that God brought me over. For this, I give Jesus all the Praise and Glory for gracing me to go through it all.

When I learn of the significance of the Mountain and what it meant; it caused me to think of the spiritual heights which the Lord have called me to. Also, the realization of the depth of Love I have for him and for myself. "I am more than a conqueror."

Therefore, on the mountain high and in the valley low experiences, I've seen the hand of God move in my Life. Therefore, this why I named my book, "Victoriously He makes all things New."
New to me exemplifies the new things that He is springing forth into my life.

However, the significance of the mountains also means love for one's self, love for the Lord, and spiritual Heights.

*How beautiful upon the mountains are the feet of him that bringeth good tidings, that publisheth peace, that bringeth good tidings of good, that publisheth salvation.*     (Isaiah 52:7).

## CONTENTS

Title Page.................................................... iv

Dedication Page.......................................... v

Epigraph..................................................... vi

Contents..................................................... vii

Acknowledgements..................................... ix

Introduction................................................ x


Chapter 1 – I am an Overcomer by the Promise of His Word .. 1

Chapter 2 – It is God's Divine Order to Protect, Guard and Guide You Until You Give Birth to Vision ............ 9

Chapter 3 – Grace is Designed to be Tailor Made for Your Life 15

Chapter 4 – Overcome Mental Bondage and Walk in Mental Freedom ................................................ 21

Chapter 5 – Don't Stop Dreaming ............................ 26

Chapter 6 – The Purpose of Oneness ....................... 34

Chapter 7 – Delivered – by the Power of Praise .......... 39

Chapter 8 – Victim to Victor .................................. 47

Chapter 9 – Wisdom Wins .................................... 53

Chapter 10 – Let Nothing Separate You from Loving One Another ....... 65

Chapter 11 – The Dynamics of Negative Words . . . . . . . . .   71

Chapter 12 – Comfort and Console .. . . . . . . . . . . . . . . . . . . ..   80

Chapter 13 – She's a Jewel . . .. . . . . . . . . . . . . . . . . . . . . . . .   87

Chapter 14 – Dynamics of Love . . . . . . . . . . . . . . . . . . . . . .   93

Chapter 15 – Seasons of Change  . . . . . . . . . . . . . . . . . . . ..   98

Chapter 16 - Victoriously He Makes All Things New ....   116


About the Author…………………………………………..   123

Retrieval Abstract…………………………………………..   125

# ACKNOWLEDGMENTS

This book has been a project for me to help all people universally to gain and maintain the victory. When I began to write it, I was in a season of brokenness, but nonetheless had victory. If I can paint a visual picture, I was in a financial drought season, I was going to therapy three times a week, and had no income. Through it all, my faith and trust increased in God and He showed me how he has made all things new through my broken season. Matthew 12:20 clarifies it, "*A bruised reed he will not break, and a smoldering wick he will not snuff out, till he has brought justice through to victory.*"

Uniquely and powerfully, I wanted to create a tool that will let people know that Victoriously - He makes all things new. Change and transformation will only come through Jesus Christ, no matter what stage of life you find yourself into. Jesus takes all negative life issues, and grants victories .... Victoriously - He makes all things new.

I appreciate the encouragement of my Mother, Mary C. Sharpton; daughters Delecia Walker and Nichelle Lee; Mentor and friend, Dr. Romelle Adams; and my church family, Nikao Life Worship Center.

Special thanks to Anointed Rose Press Publishing, for believing in me and helping me to bring this project to pass.

_ Pastor Kim Sharpton

# INTRODUCTION

<u>*Victoriously - He Makes All Things New*</u>, is a book to encourage people of all walks of life to bounce back from a place of discouragement, pain, hurt, depression, emotional distress, mental pressures and physical infirmity. I want to encourage you that the worse is over and your beginning is here. God is in the business of making all things new. I declare to you the words of the prophet Isaiah, *Behold, I will do a new thing; now it shall spring forth, and shall ye not know it? I will even make a way in the wilderness, and rivers in the desert.* (Isa. 43:19)

Your trial was a setup to bless you. Remember Mary and Martha, Lazarus' sisters, when they came to Jesus and told him that Lazarus was sick? Jesus said that his sickness was not unto death, but Lazarus died. I can imagine all the religious leaders who knew Jesus, laughing and criticizing him because of the lack of their own belief. Mary and Martha were discouraged because of the death of their brother and wept. Jesus did too. However, this death was unto the glory of God. When it seems like there's no hope or resolution to a situation to any stage of a problem, and all seems lost, God brings hope.

Martha and Mary didn't know they were in their season of miracles. God wants you to know that your desert place is about to turn into a place of hope and life for you. I declare to you this season will be a period of bounce-back for you, from everything you have experienced that caused you heartache, depression and pain, shame and tears. I declare your weeping may endure for a night, but your joy will come in the morning. I declare to you your future is blessed.

In this book, I will share some personal past experiences from my life that will show you how God has "VICTORIOUSLY" made all things new again for my life. I had some setbacks, hurts and pains, and suffered many rejections. I went through a failed marriage which ended in divorce; as well as church hurts, and physical ailments. However, the Lord has always allowed me to bounce back, and HE "Victoriously" made all things new.

Through each experience, the Holy Spirit has restored my joy, peace and love; and gave me overcoming power with a purpose-driven confidence. He is good! In all things that we suffer, we must forgive as we are forgiven.

# Chapter 1

# "I am an Overcomer by the Promise of His Word"

We will come across challenging trials and troubles as long as we are believers and living the kingdom life. Troubles will help develop our relationship with God and shape our faith; bringing our experience to a new dimension with him and into a greater place of commitment. Always, He reminds us that as long as we are in this world, we will have troubles. Don't worry about the trouble that will afflict you, because in Him He has made you and me an overcomer - John 16:33. What a great assurance that He has assured us that we are built in Him to last through the troubles and tests.

We have a victorious kind of life. Some of you may ask what "Victorious" means: Victorious is a Greek term for overcoming. It means that we have the grace to overcome whatever ills we encounter from day to day like a bad marriage, trouble with an uncontrolled child, a drug-addicted child, or a dysfunctional home. Jesus has given us (His children) a promise of victory – Psalms 34: verse 19 says, *"Many are the afflictions of the righteous, but the Lord will deliver them out of them all."* What a great promise - an agreement God made to His children. It does not matter how long your season of trial is, God promises that He will bring you out. You may be a housewife who's been afflicted in your home, and maybe your husband does not make enough to support you and your family. You may have been afflicted with a threat in your mind that you want to leave because you cannot take the fights daily. You may be that pressured business owner who is going through in your business and feel like giving up on your business due to the pressure of no sales. You may be that suffering teenager who is suffering with peer pressure in school, and doesn't know how to say "no", and wants to drop out of school due to the ongoing peer pressure. You may be that drug addict who is severely depressed because you want change to come, but you keep falling into the same slump of afflictions. I want you to know, despite what you've been going through, there *"is"* a promise manifesting and waiting to come forth - *"Many are the afflictions of the righteous, but I WILL deliver them out of them all."* As I previously said, "What an awesome promise and statement!" *"I Will"* is a factor of what He is *going* to do - it is a declaration statement of the deliverance. In other words, it *"Will"* take place. The factor is "I will deliver YOU out of all of your pains, doubts, fears, and hurts; whatever the affliction, is you WILL be brought out of it with a surety."

Now let's look at the word "Afflictions." In the Hebrew, the word afflictions is 'thlibo' which means "to suffer affliction and to be troubled". It also has reference to the sufferings due to the pressures of circumstances. We all have had sufferings that have taken us for a loop due to the pressures of life. We know those pressures will not change. Jesus said it in his word according to John 16: verse 33, *"In this world you will have trouble, but, take heart! I have overcome the world"*. The word "Overcome" means to conquer, to have control over, and to have superiority over it. Jesus points out to us that he has conquered the world and the troubles in it. Jesus makes us overcomers!

## Affliction Develops A Grace

In Acts 7: verses 9-11, because the patriarchs were jealous of Joseph, they sold him as a slave into Egypt. God was with him and rescued him from all his troubles. He gave Joseph wisdom and enabled him to gain the goodwill of Pharaoh King.

In this scripture, I want to point out the word "Jealousy". The noun for jealousy is 'zelos'. Jealousy means to envy. Joseph's brothers burned with envy toward him. They could not see him in a favored position. His father loved him the most, therefore his siblings hated him with a passion so strongly until they wanted to see him dead.

The story of Joseph was a story of great affliction, but also of grace. There was great Grace shown to Joseph from his father and God. It was not something he asked for, but it was given. For much of the time, favor can be shown to you because you are chosen by the Lord. Joseph was chosen to receive favor. It was because God could trust him with purpose and vision.

Joseph was a visionary. He carried the purpose of his family in a dream. It was not easy to expose the purpose to his family. As soon as he told what the dream was to his loved ones, immediately they despised him because of vision. Joseph already had received supplied grace first from the Spirit of God - it was the Spirit of God who gave such a revelation to Joseph concerning future events that were to occur in his life. Joseph recounted two warning dreams that led him to his greater place of grace and favor. These dreams were warning dreams that revealed his place of destiny. Joseph's dreams revealed his place of authority and leadership over his family. He told of the dreams to his brothers. He said, "Someday you all will bow down to me". Can you imagine if your siblings or child told you that someday you would bow down to them? His brothers could not stand those statements because they felt that Joseph would be superior over them. Maybe you feel like Joseph's brothers and have resentment in your heart because of where God is taking your sister or brother in Christ. He may be placing them in a leadership position over you, and you are upset because of what He is doing. My friend, I want to encourage you and tell you that He wants to destroy the bitter feeling of envy out of your heart. It is not the will of the Father that you walk with this spirit of envy and jealousy like Joseph's brothers. They went to the extreme to destroy. God is not in the destroying business, but Satan is a thief and murderer. John 10:10 says: "*The thief comes only in order to steal and kill and destroy. I came that they may have and enjoy life, and have it in abundance (to the full, until it overflows)."* The warning in the scriptures is the thief only comes to steal and kill and destroy. We know Satan's goal is to do three things in your life: to steal, to kill and to destroy.

Number 1 - To "Steal". This word steal means to take property of another wrongfully; and to come and go secretly, unobtrusively, gradually, or unexpectedly. The devil has purpose to secretly, without you knowing, take what belongs to you unexpectedly. He doesn't care about your position or place with God. He just wants what you have. Just to take your stuff. Don't be like Joseph's brothers who had Satan's character. Without notice they sought to take Joseph's life, and everything that symbolizes Christ, they tried to destroy.

### A Type Mandated for Grace

Joseph was a "type of Christ" - When you hear the statement, "A type of Christ", it speaks of something in the Old Testament which points to something in the New Testament, which is the anti-type. In Scriptures, there were many parallels between Joseph and Christ. Joseph was to be found more Christ-like in Scriptures than any other person named or found. Genesis 37: verse 12 says: *"And his brethren went to feed their father's flock in Shechem."*

Now, let's review scripture in parallels: Genesis 37: verse 3 states, *"Now Israel loved Joseph more than all his children."* (Let's note Israel was

Jacob's new name). In the first parallel, Israel loved Joseph very deeply, more than the other sons he had. Joseph is the type of the beloved son.

Jesus is the beloved Son of God. When he was baptized by John the Baptist, God spoke from heaven and said, *"This is my beloved Son, in whom I am well pleased."* (Matthew 3:17) Jesus is the anti-type, the fulfillment of the type.

In the second parallel: they both were hated by their brothers. As we read in Genesis 37: verse 4, *"When his brothers saw that their father loved him more than all his brothers, they hated him, and could not speak peaceably unto him."* Joseph's brothers despised him and did not have a kind word to say to him. The brothers of Jesus spoke sharply to him in John 7: verses 3 & 4. They rebuked him and said, *"Shew thyself to the world."* It was of a surety that Jesus' brothers despised who he was, and neither did they believe in who he was (John 7: verse 5). The accusations against Jesus and Joseph were exactly the same.

In the third parallel, they both were plotted against. For Joseph, we find in Genesis 37:20, what his brothers said, *"Come now therefore, and let us slay him."* And for Jesus, we will find in John 11:53 that the Pharisees saw Jesus as nothing but a trouble maker. But, he was the Anointed One sent to heal, deliver and transform those who could not help themselves. Let's read what the Pharisees did to Jesus. *"Then from that day forth they took counsel together for to put him to death."*

The fourth parallel is that they both were stripped of their robes. For Joseph, we read in Genesis 37: verse 23, *"And it came to pass, Joseph* was come unto his brethren that stripped Joseph out of his coat." For Jesus, we find in John 19: verse 23, *"When Jesus was crucified the soldiers took his garments and also his coat."*

In the fifth parallel, they both were taken to Egypt. For Joseph, as we read in Genesis 37: verse 28, Judah said they should sell Joseph, which they did, to a band of traveling merchants, ...and they brought Joseph into Egypt." For Jesus, as we read in Matthew 2, verse 14, when the angel told Joseph, the stepfather of Jesus, that King Herod would seek to kill the baby Jesus, *"He took the young child and his mother and departed into Egypt."*

In parallel six, my goodness, they both were sold for a price of a slave: Joseph, we read about in Genesis 37:28 verse, and we see our precious JESUS in Matthew 26 :15.

Jesus and Joseph were types in Suffering, but both were anointed to produce Grace. Yes! In all our getting, let's understand in fulfillment. We are a type and will be processed for the greater. Satan's ultimate goal is to trip God's people into a ditch of pain. Pain will always enable true victory out of the courses and challenges of life. This is called the "due process of victory". Due process gives an entitlement to pure victory because as the Devil is trying to destroy or kill you, God always sends an ambush to his plans, releasing victory.

Numbers 2 and 3 - let's look at the word "Kill", which means to "Destroy" - to put to an end and to nullify. Satan's purpose and goal is to create a trap with a solution to cause all good things for your life to come to an abrupt stop and end. You are too good for the devil to kill this way. God has planned to protect *every* valuable thing in your life. This means your health, your children, your home and everything that is connected to you.

God wants you to be kept because your position in Him is grand! Therefore, He has given angels charge over your life to protect you for the purpose of His will being manifested in your life. Whatever God has envisioned you to do, it is for His glory and no one else's. No one can stop visions and dreams from manifesting in your life, but you.

## Chapter 2

# "It is God's Divine Order to Protect, Guard, and Guide You Until You Give Birth to Vision"

Joseph had great favor, but he suffered afflictions because of the level of revelation in his life, and the enemy sought out to destroy the content of his life. Special you! YOU ARE SPECIAL. It may be so because God has destined for you to reign in His divine favor and to inherit wealth and riches from the trial that you are facing. Afflictions are purposed so He can receive praise, honor and glory from your life. Also, so you can recognize the strength in you and know that you are a gift, full of life and grace. Don't give up in the affliction of your trial, but rather give Him praise due to your development. You would not ever know how much grace you have until the enemy meets you when everything is flowing right; and then he turns everything upside down and snatches every resource that helps bring provision - you lose your job, your home is torn apart, your finances are funny, and your husband decides to leave home. All these problems determine the level of grace and blessing He is releasing in your life.

## *Grace Produces a Great Turn Around!*

One thing about grace, it always gives a great escape. When Joseph's family heard what would happen, immediately they plotted his demise. They wanted him killed, but God had a better plan. It was an escape to destiny. The game plan to destroy ended with a sure victory and purpose. Joseph did not know that his affliction developed a sure grace for him. His brothers thought they were doing him an injustice, but they were anointed to push him into the destined place allotted for him. The scriptures say in Genesis 37: verses 21-22, that Rueben persuaded them to throw Joseph with the coat his father made him into a pit, with all intentions to rescue him later from the pit. The coat of many colors that his father made for Joseph thrown in a pit by his loved ones with animal blood on top of it, was degrading but it was also grace.

Blood symbolizes life. On the Day of Atonement, a goat was used for a cause of a blood sacrifice. Also, the goat was used as a scapegoat. Usually when a sin is committed, the priest makes sacrifices using animal blood as an atonement for the soul of mankind.

Leviticus 17: verse 11 says, "*For the life of the flesh is in the blood; and I have given it to you upon the altar to make atonement for your souls.*" For it is the blood that makes atonement because of the life. *"The blood is the life".* Joseph's brothers really didn't understand the significances in the blood of the animal. What they thought they were doing was degrading him by placing blood on his coat--this act caused by his brothers was cold and hateful, but it was graceful to God. What the enemy meant for evil, God turned it around for his good. Joseph was sold into slavery by the Midianites (Genesis 37: verses 27 & 28) at the age of seventeen to Potiphar. Potiphar purchased him from the hand of the slave trader; and grace and destiny connected.

Let me explain "Grace" and "Destiny", in two-fold meanings. Grace is the favor caused by a willing act or an unwilling act. In Joseph's case, he was favored by his father. He was the eleventh child born to Jacob and Rachel. Rachel passed while giving birth to Benjamin, Joseph broke the cycle of barrenness in his mother's life, and Jacob loved Joseph because of the broken cycle of barrenness for Rachel, Joseph's mother. Joseph was loved and recognized as a miracle child. His birth revealed grace and destiny. Now Joseph is the eleventh child and his name means, "Say God add" - and God did just that! He manifested through his name. He added through his life. He added riches and honor and authority.

We are in a season of "May God add". Despite afflictions and hardships; riches and honor belong to us as His dear children, and we shall possess His authority and walk in it. Grace is nothing missing or broken from our lives. It fits us well because of the prophetic promise we have floating over our head - Nahum 1: verse 7 says, *"The Lord is good, a stronghold in the day of trouble; and he knows them that trust in him."*

Although Joseph experienced grace through his life, it did not exempt him from experiencing trauma too. Joseph's life was filled with trauma, just to explain destiny and promise to his brothers, and experience their hate toward him. To be placed in a pit and sold into slavery was traumatic. However, grace speaks loud and clear and says, just because traumatic experiences occur in your life, it does not mean you cannot experience grace and walk into your destined promise which God has revealed to you. It was a duration of twenty-two years before Joseph's dream came to pass.

Joseph was a symbolic sacrifice to his family. He had experienced much sorrow and pain through his grace process. Joseph endured separation from his beloved father (Genesis 37: verse 23), and the only family he knew. He was stripped away from him and sold into slavery to a people he did not know; but destiny was unfolding itself.

It was revelation of grace which brought him to the second part, which is" Destiny." It was such a divine connection, but it took traumatic experiences to get him there. Let me fully explain. Although you may have had bad experiences, it does not count you out of destiny and purpose. The purpose of revelation is to show you where you will be going and who you are, in authority. Many times, folks say because you may have had a bad childhood or a troubled marriage or may have been raped; that you are damaged goods and not fit for a prosperous life. The devil is a liar! That is not the case at all.

God specializes in gracing traumatic experiences. Everyone in this world is not fortunate to have a nice comfortable life without worries and problems. Joseph had problems. Many of them was because he was what you would call the "stone that was rejected". His brothers rejected him and hated who he was. Please let me say this: God wants you to embrace grace and the turmoil that is coming along with it. You may think within yourself, "I can't take the rejection, pain, hurt or hate. It's just too much." I want you to know that God has a special place in his heart for those called, misfits - He calls them his own. He loves those who are hated by the world. He has overcome everything in the world. As a matter of fact, He was hated by the world.

Your traumatic experiences are a setup for your miracle - He designed problems just to show you how powerful He is in the midst of your enemies. If Joseph would have never been through what he went through, he could not have experienced God like he did. After being sold into slavery, Joseph experienced a grace that would prosper him and the nation of Egypt - there was a multiplicity of supply for the nation of Egypt. Everything Joseph touched turned to prophetic gold. Joseph was anointed as a good steward, and Potiphar's house prospered under his supervision.

Let's take a look at Genesis 39: verses 2-5 .

Genesis 39:2 says, *"The Lord was with Joseph so that he prospered, and he lived in the house of his Egyptian master. (Verse 3) When his master saw that the Lord was with him and that the Lord gave him success in everything he did, (Verse 4), Joseph found favor in his eyes and became his attendant. Potiphar put him in charge of his household, and he entrusted to his care everything he owned."*

In Verse 5, from the time Potiphar put him in charge of his household and all that he owned, the Lord blessed the household of the Egyptians because of Joseph.

# Chapter 3

# "Grace is Designed to be Tailor-Made for Your Life"

Despite the troubles which Joseph encountered, he flowed in a grace that was tailor-made for his life. He was anointed to prosper. The scripture in Genesis 39: verse 5 says, that the Lord was with Joseph and whatever he put his hands to do, it prospered. You may ask in your mind, "How can God be with me in hard times like these?" Well, my friend, He was with Joseph, and so is He with you. Joseph experienced the hand of grace, and God never left Joseph. Although his brothers rejected him and hated him, God was with him through his process. Joseph felt in many ways like some of us. He felt fearful, confused, and angry; his emotions were shattered. He experienced what I would call emotionally traumatic experiences.

Joseph went through a great separation from his family -- eleven brothers and his father who he loved very much. He also had a plot against his life by his own family. Then, he is placed in a pit with his coat that his father made for him, symbolizing his love and favor for his son. The coat is destroyed by animal blood. Know that God divinely moves and gives Joseph a favor that would cause a nation to prosper. You and I are like Joseph, the rejected stone. Problems seem to persist in almost every part of our lives but, unexpectedly, God grants us a grace that will take us into a destiny. God's ways are perfect, illuminating our paths. He knows the directions that He is taking us as His people. Don't complain when unseemly things happen. Just rejoice and tell God "thank you" for your tailor-made grace.

### *Grace in Action*

Joseph still encountered problems that would later become a teacher through grace. It was in action for his life. In Genesis 39: verses 6-7, the scriptures say, *"So Potiphar left everything he had in Joseph's care."* With Joseph in charge, he did not concern himself with anything except the food he ate.

Now Joseph was well built and handsome. After a while, his master's wife took notice of Joseph in charge and said, *"Come to bed with me!"* Here it was - Joseph had everything. He was in charge. His boss put him in charge of his house - he was in authority. Why would she do that to Joseph? This problem was sent by the devil. Evil enticement was designed for Joseph to lose his position in his master's house. Joseph ran for his life. There is a song called, "I Am Running for My Life." *(If anyone asks you what is the matter with me, just tell them that I am saved, and I am sanctified, Holy Ghost filled and fire-baptized. I have Jesus on my side and I am running for my life.)* This is what we will have to do when sin comes to catch us in a net. We <u>must</u> run and understand that God has a greater plan for our lives.

Sin is nothing but a death sentence for us. The scripture in Romans 6: verse 23 says, *"For the wages of sin is death."* Satan is the author of sin. God does not cause sin, Satan does, and he makes it look really good, so you will fall into it and never come out. It is his design to destroy "Your" purpose and future, for good. Better than that, God has something greater and He is waiting for us to yield to His plan of action for our lives. The plan of action is the <u>avoiding of sin</u> and <u>receiving of favor</u>. Sin motivates the heart to <u>ignore</u> God's plan to bless. The blessing God has designed to give us will only come when our flesh will yield and obey His voice.

You may be in a sinful relationship right now and don't want to move out of it because you are benefiting from it. The person may be paying your bills, buying your clothing and keeping a roof over your head. You may feel empty on the inside. The reason is because God is calling you to be free from sin and bondage. "Sin" causes heavy problems, and Satan is the head of sin. It is he that brings heavy bondage into our lives, leaving us empty and full of fear and doubt; and sometimes blaming God for the problems that have come into your lives. Sin is easy to get into, but hard to get out of. So, for those who are running from sin, continue to run and stay faithful "to the Lord".

Genesis 39: verse 8 says, *"but he refused."* He refused what was presented to him -- a web of betrayal, lies, and deceit. Had Joseph sinned with his master's wife, he would have been sinning against the Lord. Just think who you are sinning against when sin presents itself; remember the goodness God gives to you as his beloved child. It is more than just a fornication act or an adulterous affair. He is the redeemer of all mankind and a rewarder to man for their faithfulness to Him. Grace is always in action for His people.

Again, let's take a look at the trials that took place and the grace that moved on Joseph's behalf. Had Joseph sinned, he would have breached the trust between him and his master, so he ran from the temptation presented. The climax of seduction from Potiphar's wife came on the day when she tried to seduce Joseph. No one else was around to witness the act. After he turned her down, he began to take flight, running to get away from her. She grabbed his clothes and blamed him for an act that would cause him to lose everything. She lied to cover up her seduction, and he suffered a major setback behind what she did.

Many can bear witness to what lies can do to your life. A lie can put you in the chamber of failure. I know many people who have lost everything due to un-truths, such as their marriages, friends, children, and jobs. I declare to you, despite the lies that were destined to trap you and zap your life, YOU HAVE THE VICTORY!

Let me define the word "Lie" in this context.

Lie (pseudo) means "a falsehood- the purpose being to deceive people into the acknowledgement of the spurious claim to deity on the part of the man of sin.

Joseph was locked up for a lie. John 8:44-45 describes well the lies told by Satan. John says, *"You belong to your father; the devil and you want to carry out your father's desires. He was a murderer from the beginning, not holding to the truth for there is no truth in him."* (John 8:44)

### A liar will destroy your life.

Let's take an account of what Joseph encountered. Potiphar's wife lied on him and said he tried to rape her. She used a piece of his clothing against him that she tore from his body as evidence to trap him in a lie. Joseph's life was filled with crisis, blame, hurt, pain and blessings. He went from hatred of his brothers to the lies that landed him in prison.

He faced trauma, but blessings too. God added manifold blessings to him. Some people know what it is to be hated among loved ones, but also know what it feels like to be lied on. You may be going through this very test that almost cost you your freedom - mental freedom, physical freedom and emotional freedom.

# Chapter 4

# "Overcome Mental Bondage and Walk in Mental Freedom"

"Mental bondage" is when your mind is entangled with thoughts due to heavy circumstances you may be faced with. Let's take an assessment of Joseph's life. Due to the separation from his family, and to his brothers putting him in a pit; it left his mind with thoughts of fear. What is "Fear?" According to Webster's dictionary, fear is defined as: sudden danger, attempt of peril, fright, alarm or panic, trepidation, which means painful agitation in the presence or anticipation of danger, to lose courage.

I would like to speak a little bit on mental bondage. Confusion will come in when a situation does not make logical sense; like what Joseph went through. It did not make logical sense and it caused mental confusion to set in. How many of us have gone through heightened trials that did not make sense to us and threw our mind into mental confusion? Things happen without reason. "Why?" some of us may question. Let me answer this question for you. It is because God has favored you out of the rest to go through a test that may cause a nation to be saved. It is the mental battle that causes progress to be slowed down; meaning if the devil can get your mind off focus, then he can steal what God desires for you to have. If our minds aren't transformed, we will not be able to process the gate of victory in the spirit of our minds. Your mind must not be stagnated in the cause of healing and growth; but you must renew the spirit of your mind. It is very imperative that you do so. The mental renewing process starts with (Romans 12:2) and with the daily word alignment. Meditating on the word and allowing it to renew your mind is called a mental process, on the road to healing  Also, practicing the word of God, speaking it, and meditating on it until it manifests what it says.

## *Overcome emotional bondage and walk in emotional freedom*

Like Joseph, I have been through some situations that laid heavy on my emotions. I was in a situation on my job. I was in a position that I did not like. I continued to apply for internal positions, but they would always look over me and pick other people for the position. There was a glass ceiling. I began to hold resentment and hurt and became angry because I knew I was being overlooked. I had the education and qualifications, plus the experience, but they would not hire me for the position I applied for. I was upset because I was wronged. For months, I wondered why they did not pick me for any of the positions I applied for. Later, I learned the supervisor I worked under was jealous of me because I had degrees and she did not have any. She worked tirelessly against me to stop my progress on my job.

Emotional Freedom - emotional bondage is when your emotions are not free due to hurt, pain, and resentment from a bad circumstance. The circumstance could have been a bad marriage, a troubled home, sibling rivalry, or a church matter. This situation could have an effect on the way you process your emotions and view relationships. Emotional healing is very important, especially when it deals with your personal life and determination in all life purposes.

If you don't get free from emotional bondage, you'll never experience the dominion power that is promised to you from the word of God in Luke 10:19, which says, *"Behold! I have given you authority and power to trample upon serpents and scorpions, and {physical and mental strength and ability} over all the power that the enemy {possesses}; and nothing shall in any way harm you."* The word gives us a clear description of the dominion-power given to the believer - it's clear to me that we have dominion over our emotional health and can conquer everything the enemy brings to us because we have power over it.

## *Overcome Physical bondage and Walk in Physical freedom*

Galatians 5:1-21 In {this} freedom, Christ has made us free {and has completely liberated us}; stand fast then, and do not be hindered and held ensnared and submit again to a yoke of slavery {which you have once put off}.

<u>Physical freedom</u>- Physical freedom enables the believer to walk free from physical issues due to life circumstances. Physical bondage is a yoke of slavery which will cause the believer to live in a manner of slavery in the flesh. The believer becomes chained to envying, murders, drunkenness, reveling, and the like. These are fleshly bondages the flesh longs for. I must emphasize the importance of walking in the Spirit that will help destroy the habitual lust that will come to engage the mind, emotions and the body. The Holy Spirit helps build hope and confidence in us to walk and live in Him to nullify all fleshly cravings that will stop us from being free in Him.

The provision of freedom is when you can come to grips that who the SON sets free is free indeed, and what the pure manifestation of it is. Your life is meant to influence in a positive sense which will cause freedom for others. When your life exposes what Christ did for you, then you will experience pure joy from the Holy Spirit. Then those around you will experience freedom just by reading your life through your personal testimony.

<u>John 8:36</u>:

*"So, if the Son sets you free, you will be free indeed."* This scripture gives a clear and precise explanation of freedom in Jesus. I want to declare to you; the Son comes to set you free. I don't care what has come to bind you, to stop you and cause you to feel like you have no victory. Your victory

and freedom are locked in the Son; who is the Son of Righteousness and who has your healing in His wings! There is no question about His healing which WILL COME TO BRING JUSTICE IN EVERY AREA OF YOUR LIFE. Glory to God! Yes, healing justifies you in the place where the devil declares you guilty of Sin. God is having mercy to release you into a place of freedom from hurts, bad decisions, lost hopes and dreams. The Son of righteousness restores your heart from the pitfalls of devastation. The Healing in His wings provides love, joy and peace from the Son who enlightens with great hope for tomorrow. *"Never allow your yesterday problems to collide with your hopes and dreams for today. BOUNCE BACK"* – Kim D. Sharpton

Problems will come into our lives back to back, but the plan in action is the grace which moves us quickly into harmony with destiny. Joseph was designed to prosper a nation through drought. Drought would seem to be devastating when people around you look to you - hopeless and dreamless because they don't know what tomorrow may bring. Devastation sometimes can kill your dream, or it can make you move in hope to bring your dream to pass.

# Chapter 5

# "Don't Stop Dreaming"

Let your dreams take you into your purpose. Let's define dreams: Dreams are supernatural transmissions of visions; insights given by the Father through the Holy Spirit as revelations which communicate through your sleep, activities, sentiments or desire. Dreams are birthed mentally. They begin as submerged thoughts, ideas or activities which are birthed and buried within the dreamer. The Lord sends messages through his prophetic dream angel to reveal information - past, present or future.

Genesis 28:10-22

Jacob left Beersheba and set out for Haran. [11] When he reached a certain place, he stopped for the night because the sun had set. Taking one of the stones there, he put it under his head and lay down to sleep. [12] He had a dream in which he saw a stairway resting on the earth, with its top reaching to heaven, and the angels of God were ascending and descending on it. [13] There above it stood the Lord, and he said, *"I am the Lord, the God of your father Abraham and the God of Isaac. I will give you and your descendants the land on which you are lying.* [14] *Your descendants will be like the dust of the earth, and you will spread out to the west and to the east,* *to the north and to the south. All peoples on earth will be blessed through you and your offspring. <sup>15</sup> I am with you and will watch over you wherever you go, and I will bring you back to this land. I will not leave you until I have done what I have promised you."*

This dream occurred during a troublesome time and Jacob needed to hear from the Lord. So, he went to Bethel and built an altar to take counsel of the Lord. The Lord heard from him and answered Jacob by a dream.

A transmission was downloaded from heaven through his mental process. The Lord downloaded purpose and destiny of future to him. He gave him a prophetic dream that would change the course of his life.

God gave Jacob blessings and told him of the future destination for his offspring, and of protection. The Lord spoke to tell Jacob, "The land you are on is yours." Let's remember who the land originally belonged to. It belonged to the Canaanites, but now it's Jacob's. The Word of God said He will give you houses and land that you never build on.

Joshua 24:13

*"I gave you land you had not worked on, and I gave you towns you did not build--the towns where you are now living. I gave you vineyards and olive groves for food, though you did not plant them."*

This land belonged to the Canaanites, the descendants of Cain. Remember Cain who slew his brother Abel and was cursed because of it.

His descendants were rich people but did not love God. The Canaanites were a wicked people who worshipped idols. They did not love The Lord of Lords. They did evil in the sight of the Almighty God, but they had riches which were good for Israel. *"A good man leaveth an inheritance to his children's children: and the wealth of the sinner is laid up for the just"* (Proverbs 13:22).

It is a fact when God's word explains that we will have wealth and riches from the sinners. It means those who do not deserve wealth and grace shall not have it. But the glorious transfer of wealth will be given to His sons and daughters. In this end-time, it seems like everything is drying up and seems like what belongs to us is being denied. You must remember what I said earlier in the chapter, it's all about principles. The fundamentals: What is given as a teaching tool that shall be put to practice? You may be like Jacob, who just needs to hear from the Lord, or needs riches and blessings on your offspring. Your breakthrough will come when you decide to build an altar and die to you, so you can hear from the Lord.

### Wealth transfer

The Canaanites' wealth went to Jacob who Loved God. *"Your offspring will be like the dust of the earth. They will be in the east, west, north and south."* This prophecy was spoken to Abraham and now reaffirmed to Jacob.

Genesis 13:16

*"I will make your offspring like the dust of the earth: so that if anyone could count the dust, then your offspring could be counted."*

This promise consisted of two nations, the Jewish and the Arab nation. Sarai, Abraham's wife, brought forth the Jewish nation; and Hagar, Sarai's handmaiden, brought forth the Arab nation. Genesis 17:20.

In the Book of Genesis, the story is clear of the Ishmael blessing. The story gives a clear view on the angelic visitation in which he meets Hagar. Let's remember the covenant was to be established through Sarai; the established promise was to come through Isaac, for Israel is God's Chosen people.

Let's look into the generational line of the two nations. Sarai was a Hebrew, chosen to carry the lineage of the Israel nation - such a great and valuable task. Meanwhile, she doubts what God says to her, concerning the promise. This is such a mistake that many of us have when we are spoken to by the Holy Ghost concerning our destiny. We laugh and doubt all at the same time, not believing what God can do in our barren situation.

Let's take account with Sarai. She was barren. To be barren is to be unfruitful, unproductive and desolate. When you don't bring forth in the Jewish custom, you are looked upon as useless. Many today are in a barren situation. You are not fruitful on your job, your marriage is not yielding seed, your churches are unfruitful concerning souls, and all seems lost and hopeless. Your life is unjoyful and you're looking for a breakthrough to break out inside your life.

Like Sarai, the promise which was spoken seemed not to manifest during the time she wanted it to. There was no life behind the promise. She waited until she could not wait any more. She laughed at her husband, blaming her doubt on old age; but really, was it that she had lost hope in herself? She was locked on a promise that seemed not to come to pass in her time. She looked at her handmaid, Hagar, to carry her promise. What Sarai did not understand was the Jewish lineage was being pure and not to be combined with any other bloodline.

Also, Israel was told not to intermarry with other nations because of their beliefs. The Lord knew his beloved nation of people's hearts would be influenced away from the Lord. The Lord, wanting a sweet communion with his beloveds, didn't want them to serve other beliefs that would cloud their judgment of the true and living God. In 1 Kings 11:2, they were from nations about which the LORD had told the Israelites, *"You must not intermarry with them, because they will surely turn your hearts after their gods. Nevertheless, Solomon held fast to them in love."* God chose Israel out of all nations because of the promise made to Abraham, which deemed them blessed out of all nations.

### Deuteronomy 7:7-9

*7It was not because you were more in number than any other people that the Lord set his love on you and chose you, for you were the fewest of all peoples, 8 but it is because the Lord loves you and is keeping the oath that he swore to your fathers, that the Lord has brought you out with a mighty hand and redeemed you from the house of slavery, from the hand of Pharaoh king of Egypt. ⁹ Know therefore that the Lord your God is God, the faithful God who keeps covenant and steadfast love with those who love him and keep his commandments, to a thousand generations."*

John 15:16 -- *"You didn't choose me. I chose you. I appointed you to go and produce lasting fruit, so that the Father will give you whatever you ask for, using my name."*

As the Lord puts his stamp of approval on your life, he gives you blessings, houses and lands. He increases your generations and counts them worthy of blessing because you've been found faithful. He also gives favor and protection to you and your family all the days of your life because you take counsel of Him. The Lord passes down blessings from your mother and father to you and your generation. He is faithful who promises. Who deems such blessings as the Father simply because you allow your flesh to die on the altar? Often when an altar is built to take counsel of the Lord, it is for the result of dying so the Spirit will have free course in a person's life. What a magnificent strategy the Lord gives to a person as He has need of them. To build an altar to alter some things in their life. It does not matter what the devil will try to do to you, God's plan and purpose for your life will be victorious, and full of blessings and fulfilled promises.

What Jacob did was position himself for the blessings. The principles laid out are simple: Jacob built an altar, so he could receive revelation from the Lord. I can say altering is not a bad thing. It only means, what God is going to do, will only fit you. You will be the only one to receive prophecy because it's just for you. Don't you love blessings just for you? After God blest Jacob, Jacob blest God for all he did. Jacob's heart was grateful, so he blest God for the revelation, the wealth transfer, and the land of Canaan. The Lord was faithful in all He did. He understood the principle of the altar. Many times, when you bury yourself into your struggles before the blessings come, you should get excited because after struggle comes blessings. Principles are put in place as a guide to follow and apply to one's life – a teaching tool.

Let's remember what a "Principle" is: a principle is a fundamental truth put in place for learning and growth. This means every underlying principle is put in place for fundamental purpose, so we can grow by it. Had Jacob not built an altar, he would not have received revelation, simply but sure? Principles also give messages. The Lord's messages to Jacob was, "Lay before me and I will show you and speak to you." In the dream, God's way of dealing with Jacob was visual and audible. The Lord showed him and spoke to him two-fold, seeing and hearing. Jacob saw ladders in the dream which took him to the throne room, and the heavens were opened. The Psalmist said in Psalm 144:5, *"Bow thy heavens, O Lord, and come down"*. The angels ascending and descending showed the entrance and angels around the throne of God, and then the presence of God was revealed.

How hungry are you to receive God? How hungry are you to read His divine truths which release blessings upon your life? That sounds like heaven on earth. Well, my friend, it's your time for revelation; God's revealed presence, which speaks to your need. Obstacles, hardships, or separations will never shut God out of your life. As long as you remember His purpose and principles, while praying and dying to you in the process - He will show you and speak to you.

# Chapter 6

# *"The Purpose of Oneness"*

In John 16:33 (KJV), Jesus Christ said, *"These things I have spoken unto you, that in me ye might have peace. In this world ye shall have tribulation: but be of good cheer; I have overcome the world."* Jesus is right that we will have trouble in this world. Trouble is everywhere. There is hardly a person who is not affected by trials and troubles. Why should His followers who live on earth take heart or have courage because He has overcome? One can say it's fine for you Jesus that you have overcome the world. I haven't, and I am suffering for it. The reason Jesus gave is seen in the scriptures; that we are one with Christ.

When we received God's grace, that grace made us to become sons of God. As a result of that, we are one with Christ Jesus. Understanding our oneness with Jesus is very important in understanding God's grace to us. God's grace that made us one with Jesus also empowers us to overcome challenges as Jesus did. That's why Paul was able to say, *"I can do all things through Christ who strengthens me."* (Philippians 4:13)

Because Jesus lived in him and he lived in Jesus, Paul and Jesus were spiritually one. Jesus not only strengthened him, but also endured with him. In the same way, when Paul talked about his labor in the work of God, he ascribed that to God's grace working in him (1 Corinthians 15:10). That grace was Jesus Christ living in him and working in him by the Holy Spirit.

The scriptures also demonstrate our oneness with Jesus in many other ways. We are called the body of Christ and the bride of Christ. It is the unity and the bond of covenant which Christ wants to demonstrate through every marriage, and to show how He loves us. God is the author of marriage! The beauty of the aspect of life in every stage is that God thinks of man's longings and desire and fulfills them.

In the beginning of ages, God spoke into existence by His creative power which manifested at the power of His words. The Lord spoke, *"Let there be light",* and light came into the earth. Genesis 1:14 -- *"And God said, "Let there be lights in the vault of the sky to separate the day from the night and let them serve as signs to mark sacred times, and days and years, 15 and let them be lights in the vault of the sky to give light on the earth." And it was so. 16 God made two great lights—the greater light to govern the day and the lesser light to govern the night. He also made the stars. 17 God set them in the vault of the sky to give light on the earth, 18 to govern the day and the night, and to separate light from darkness. And God saw that it was good."*

So, as earth longed to have light, the Lord filled the longing of insight. No longer did darkness fade the light. As well, as the longing heart and aloneness of man to long for companionship, the Father fills the longing soul of man. It was never the designed plan of the Father to have man in the earth by himself without help. As the Father's thoughts filled the earth, man's blueprint of destiny was put in place.

God, in his infinite wisdom, calls man into being. Adam His son, the first man to be called into existence, was created from the dust of the earth (Genesis 2:7). He didn't come by way of water or blood as like the only begotten son, JESUS (John 3: verse 16 and 1 John 5: verses 6, 7 and 8). Let's keep in mind that I am speaking of Adam. However, he fulfills <u>nature's</u> first mandate. Marriage, then family! It's so exciting how our heavenly Father teaches us through life's examples of marriage that you can't be one by yourself.

*Genesis 1:* [26] *Then God said, "Let us make mankind in our image, in our likeness, so that they may rule over the fish in the sea and the birds in the sky, over the livestock and all the wild animals, and over all the creatures that move along the ground.*

[27] *So God created mankind in his own image, in the image of God he created them; male and female he created them."*

[28] *God blessed them and said to them, "Be fruitful and increase in number; fill the earth and subdue it. Rule over the fish in the sea and the birds in the sky and over every living creature that moves on the ground."*

As we read in Genesis 1:26-27, it shows how God ordained man and woman to be one. He created man in His own image and gave them purpose. The Lord made an agreement with the two of them to be fruitful, to fill the earth, to subdue it, and to rule in unity and power over everything together. What I love is that the Lord put both of them over the earth, not just one (Genesis 1: verses 27 and 28).

Before trouble began in the earth realm, the ultimate plan was for man and woman to walk in the behavior of oneness. Let me explain and define "Oneness"; to emerge mentally, emotionally, physically and socially. When two people enter into marriage, they become one flesh. In understanding the Word of God, the mandate is given to man and woman, which goes beyond any other relationship and union. It is the righteousness from the Lord; the making of two becoming one. It's a very unique factor, but holy, wholesome and healthy.

Now, I am going to explain the simplicity of this mandate for man and woman. The decree of marriage notes that man and woman become deemed as healthy partners under the law of God. Then, it is to work under God's divine construction, which legalizes man and woman to become lovers. Man is given instructions to leave home and be joined to his wife and they shall become one. Man would have never thought that the sexual communication between two would bring the mysterious union of oneness into marriage. Oh my! Such righteousness of love - wholesome and holy which breathes life.

As I continue on later in Chapter 8, I will discuss more about the marriage relationship, which will help you gain more insight and wisdom of marriage and the divine purpose of the marital relationship.

# Chapter 7

# "Delivered – By the Power of Praise"

David had a testimony. He had a blessed life because he knew who God was. His exaltation and praise of thanksgiving brought him to a greater place of redemption.

David never took his eyes off the Lord. He had many deliverances and brushes with death, and he had a story of the magnificent grace and power of God. His tenacity of dance and his uplifting sound of praise brought life to those that surrounded him. David understood the conquering power of his Heavenly King. The Psalmist received personal provision, life saving grace, and favor from his God. He exalted God in the midst of hardships. David lived victoriously because he put God first even when he came head on with death. His praise was, "Had it not been for the Lord on my side."

Psalm 124

*If the Lord had not been on our side—*
*let Israel say—*
*if the Lord had not been on our side*

*when people attacked us,*
*they would have swallowed us alive*
*when their anger flared against us;*
*the flood would have engulfed us,*
*the torrent would have swept over us,*
*5 the raging waters*
*would have swept us away.*

*6 Praise be to the Lord,*
*who has not let us be torn by their teeth.*
*7 We have escaped like a bird*
*from the fowler's snare;*
*the snare has been broken,*
*and we have escaped.*
*8 Our help is in the name of the Lord,*
*the Maker of heaven and earth.*

In the midst of trouble, we have to praise God despite what is seen around us. In all occasions, praise is the proper response to problems. It causes a high volume of breakthrough when problems get rough and it seems there is no way out. "Praise" always suits every case because it assures true Victory!

In some of my life experiences, only praise assured me victory. I can remember early on in my walk with Christ, I struggled with not having money. Yes! I had money problems. I was facing an eviction. I owed so much money, I did not know where I was going to get money from to pay my debts. Well, I began to get on my knees and call upon the name of the Lord. As I continued to pray, the Spirit of the Lord fell upon me and all I could do was to give the highest praise, "Hallelujah! Thank you, Jesus. Lord I love you." I then had an Assurance that it was worked out; a turnaround was on its way. It was the power of my "praise" that determined the magnitude of my Victory. Just then, I overcame my fear of being evicted from my apartment.

David faced the same fears as we do: the loss of a loved one, troubles within the family circle, his children, problems with his flesh, outside rivalries and at times he had to run for his life. Saul, David's mentor, who taught him almost everything he knew of the skill of war became envious of David when the Lord allowed him to conquer his wars, because he put the Lord first.

Saul hated the fact that David killed tens of thousands and he only killed thousands. His heart was perverted with hatred and he hated David because David knew how to call upon the name of the Lord and get a response. David experienced the hand of God moving on his behalf releasing victory. David loved the Lord and obeyed Him and sought to please Him.

Saul tormented David because of his abilities and the position he had with God. David praised his way through adversity. His whole heart was dedicated with respect, honor and gratefulness. His mindset and body were yielded despite his circumstances. He understood the principle of praise as a declaration of celebration. David used his trial as a declaration to celebrate and rejoice in his victory. Without reservation, he then took authority over his situation and gave God a victorious praise for coming out of his situation. With his breath he praised, with his hands he praised, and with his feet he danced in celebration.

2 Samuel 6:14 –And David danced before the Lord with all his might, wearing a priestly garment."

He celebrated the goodness of the Lord in the land of the living by lifting his feet in thanks, leaping for joy in appreciation for all the great things the Master did for him. David's rejoicing was signature of deliverance for breakthrough.

King Saul, the first king asked for by the nation of Israel, was not God's choice, but God granted it because they wanted a king. This Saul, king of Israel, represents disobedience, rebellion and outright defiance. How many of us have, or has had, a Saul in your life? A hater - one who could not see the favor of God operating in full in your life? Your hater represents the spirit of Saul, one that rebels against the presence of God, and who walks in dry places due to disobedience towards our heavenly King. Your hater despises you because he or she sees the fulfillment of purpose required to lead a people from glory to glory. It's not your fault that you have the key and the anointing that will break barriers and bring change into peoples' lives everywhere. You may not understand this level of trial, but just put a praise on it, because it's your praise that will cause a great breakout of victory! It is your praise which brings greater purpose to your situation and others around you. Yes! It causes joy in the midst of depression and hurt. Your praise applauds the Lord for breaking barriers, healing the broken and giving strength to the weak.

**"Your Praise is full of purpose which propels those who are committed, to breaking out against all odds"** – Kim D. Sharpton.

Praise is the benefactor and the driving force which determines greater benefits from the Lord. In other words, praise will bring you into a sphere of influence and miracles. When you discover that God's breaking point for your life is for you to lift Him up and magnify Him; then you will be persuaded that you will succeed through praise. Oh my! There is great hope and confidence in knowing how to lift the Master up in praise. Fred Hammond, the singer and songwriter wrote the song, "When the Spirit of the Lord." He wrote the song in celebration and rejoicing of what the Lord did for David. The lyrics go like this: *"When the Spirit of the Lord comes upon my heart, I will dance like David danced. I will dance, dance, dance like David danced."* God intends for you to "dance" in your victory and know that your greatest breakthroughs will come through your dance. Kingdoms and territories are brought down to nothing through praise and submitting to the Holy Ghost.

You are built to win! You were never purposed to lose. In every level of warfare, the "Lord" releases strategy so you can win! In David's case, it was a rock and sling shot and praise. In your case, it's simple instruction from the Lord. Without exploring those simple instructions, you will never learn the heights to win your battles. David was a kingdom player and learned how to obey God through his suffering and battles. Let me propose this question to you. What are you learning in your suffering? Are you still in the same slump going through the same trial and testing and have not learned anything from your pain? Every round goes higher but will take you into a level of teaching. You must learn that your test becomes a blackboard of teaching. Your heart is open, and wisdom is the writer of experience. Experience produces character, character gives hope and makes you not ashamed in anything because the excellency of it all is Victory.

David was a kingdom player. He moved in obedience toward God. On one occasion of the psalms, a mighty remarkable deliverance was about to take place for the nation of Israel. It was around the Persian period when David was face on with his son Absalom, who was rebellious and hateful towards his father. This psalm of David gives us rare insight into the early peril of his kingdom, particularly from the Philistines; who had thought to see the last of Israel when they shattered the kingdom of Saul.

2 Samuel 5:17 - gives a clear view of the severity of the threat and how little confidence David placed in his own power to survive them. The Philistines had plans to raid to gain territory, and to put an end to David and the hope of Israel. Maybe you feel like David who lacked confidence in winning his battles. I want to encourage you that you are not a victim, but a victor in all circumstances. In some situations, the volume of the threats is louder and higher than others, and it may seem like your confidence is not strong. I want you to know you will never fulfill your position if you are in the wrong place in your faith. God designed that your faith will produce life over fear because fear produces death. Anyone who does not believe

will never produce hope and trust in God. Therefore, you can never please Him.

Hebrews 11:6 - *"And without faith, it is impossible to please God, because anyone who comes to Him must believe that He exists and that rewards who earnestly seek Him."* Trespass of position will always cause troubles and will lead to destruction. Our position in this life is to find out our place. Where do we belong? We are never meant to be a victim but a victor. Victoriously, our assignment causes us to be brought into newness. Hallelujah!

In my book, *"$167.50, My Price for Freedom"*, I wrote my story of loss, pain, hurt, victory and freedom. In one stage of my life, I was a victim. The Lord showed me that all was not lost. I had to see through the pressure of loss and overcome the negative pursuits which were purposed to take my life over. I made it through the shadows of death, which was vital for me to live. Yes! I am an overcomer. Overcoming was my benefit to purpose, and purpose gave me wisdom to know victory was mine. I had to tell every storm to go the other way, so I could live.

I am not a victim to life hurts, pains and persecutions; but it comes as a revelation of a mental picture of victory. You may be feeling defeated as you are reading this book. Let me explain to you. Feeling downhearted is normal, especially when you are in a storm. Remember, storms always can be calmed and spoken to. You have the power to speak to every obstacle in life and defeat has to go, low self-esteem has to go, pain has to go and wrong decision making has to go. It is up to you to use the power that is in you that will help you gain victory. In the next chapter, I explain how I moved from being a victim to a victor.

# Chapter 8

# "Victim to Victor"

*"He who finds a wife finds what is good and receives favor from the Lord"* - Proverbs 18:22.

I was very happy and excited to get married, but there was a level of warfare coming against the marriage. Before we could get married, there were all types of confusion. His family was telling him not to marry me and my family was telling me not to marry him. I was so upset because I really could not understand. One day I was on my way to the church for rehearsal and I heard the precious Holy Spirit say to me, "Don't marry him. Wait on me". He spoke the second time and said, "Wait on me". I sat there stunned. I didn't't know what to think or do. Here the Lord was speaking to me a command not to marry, to wait!

All my money was out. I had paid for everything: the cake, the ladies' dresses, my gown, and the church rental. Here it was I was about to be married in twenty-four hours. I was troubled; I thought to myself how can I tell this man what the Holy Spirit said to me without him getting upset?

We were in love, so I went on with my plans to marry. The wedding was small, very quiet but joyful. We could not afford too much because we both had limited resources. We had a blended family and we did not want to spend a lot on a wedding, knowing we had to live afterwards.

Marriage is a mandate from God. It was created for man and woman to be fruitful and multiply in the earth. Yet, I find it real confusing, and I wonder because many rush to make their way to the altar. Then on the other hand, many want out. I find that one of the most cherished, and then difficult, of all relationships is the importance of marriage. Marriage can be the most enjoyable and rewarding of all relationships.

Man's sole satisfying need, outside of God, is woman. *"So, the Lord God caused the man to fall into a deep sleep; and while he was sleeping, he took one of the man's ribs, and then closed up the place with flesh. Then the Lord God made a woman from the rib he had taken out of the man, and he brought her to the man. The man said, "This is now bone of my bone and flesh of my flesh; she shall be called woman, for she was taken out of man.""* Adam identified her position as the woman in his life. Eve completed Adam. In essence, in his completion, she made him feel whole, lacking nothing as far as relationship. That is why a man leaves his father and mother and is united to his wife, and they become one flesh. (Gen 2:20-24).

Man has a sole satisfying need to be married. Remember the Lord said that it was not good for man to be alone; 'I will make him a helper suitable for him.' The word helper or helpmate originates from the Hebrew term, a help or agreement, to him. This means a woman is designed to be an appropriate helper for man. She is well-matched with him – morally, mentally, emotionally, and physically. She is his balance, improving what he lacks and fulfilling his potential. For she is the one God brings to the man to help bring out his potential. She is the one who will help give him favor with the Lord. She is the one that will come between him and the Lord when He gets angry with him for his disobedience.

Before I got married, I asked God to send me an appeasing type of man of God. One who would be a spiritual head to me, a good father and example to my children and a good provider. It is God's good pleasure to bless his daughters with good men to have fruitful relationships.

The bible says, God brought Eve to Adam (Genesis 2: verse 23). It is something when God prepares his sons and daughters for their mates. He not only prepares you but brings you to him. It is something here because Adam didn't find Eve. The bible says that Eve was brought to man. Women, when God wants to bring someone into your lives, you first must fix yourselves up, put on the finest of clothing, place on good smelling perfume and lay at his feet, positioning yourselves for his proposal. Boaz saw Ruth's humility, strength and tenacity. She was ready to be taken. She understood servanthood and what it took for her to be his wife. Out of all the rest of the women, she was beautiful in his eyes.

Woman is a part of man. Man makes the mistake when he thinks that there is no equality between them both. I can carefully say that God created both equal in the sense of humanity, not order. Woman is not a second-class citizen in humanity. The bible teaches in 1 Corinthians Chapter 11: verse 3 – *"But I would have you know, that the head of every man is Christ; and the head of the woman is the man; and the head of Christ is God."* Now divine order was put in place by God himself. This does not mean man is to abuse his wife, or abandon his wife, or not to provide for his wife. This simply means that Christ has made him fully responsible for the family as the natural and spiritual head. He is to lead the family spiritually to God, and he is to lay a biblical foundation and live according to the word of God too.

**I am not defeated- but victorious.**

Genesis 2: verses 23-24 says the man said, *"This is now bone of my bones and flesh of my flesh; she shall be called woman, for she was taken out of man.* Marriage is a defining role of the church, and clear perspectives should be underlined in the marriage role. Too many married couples are walking and living defeated in the church simply because "Christ" is not the center of the marriage. If there is another purpose of how the marriage should function, then I believe the statistics would be lower on this matter.

Before the Marriage Covenant is entered into, Biblical Counseling should be sought! Counseling is so IMPORTANT *before* the marriage covenant is entered into. For some couples, new marriages can be rigid mentally, emotionally, internally, and economically. Sometimes the coping mechanism can become shallow and instead of the married couple seeking counseling, they seek a way out of the marriage, as if there is no hope. So, in other words, we don't give our marriages a try when we have already made up in our minds we want out, instead of allowing Christ, the ultimate healer, to heal what might be broken. Tragedy comes in any relationship with a couple, especially when the male as the spiritual head over the wife and home, does not try to fix what might be broken.

Marriage is a task. When two people come into the marriage, they come in with two different views and mindsets on how relationships are to be. For instance, when I got married, I came from a broken home. My Mom and Dad were divorced when I was young. From the little I did remember, Dad worked at a bakery and Mom worked too, as a Nurse assistant. All along, the family structure of the home was breaking down. Dad did his dirt and Mom worked hard. Dad stayed home but did his dirt while he was home.

Life in marriage is responsibility to God first, and then to the family. Many marriages are broken because husbands and wives do not want to take full responsibility for their actions for themselves. In relationships, marriages can survive hardships if the husband and wife would allow "Christ" to rule over their hearts.

Let me explain. When the Holy Spirit is in control over your heart, it is guarded with the word of God. In the word of God, David says, *"It's your word that I hide in my heart that I might not sin against thee.* (Psalms 119: verse 11.) Having the word in your heart will prevent double-mindedness. Having a double-mind will, in fact, create conflict. It's like having two minds. A mind that wants to do worldly things, and then a spiritual mind that wants the Lord. This type of mind is called "double-minded" or "split mind." This is why James 1: verse 8, says: *"A double-minded man is unstable in all of his ways"*. A marriage that has a double-minded husband or wife will never thrive in victory. The normality of a victorious marriage is a stable marriage with direction and a plan to go through storms and tests of life together.

James 3: verse 17 says: *"But the wisdom from above is first of all pure (undefiled); then it is peace - loving, courteous (considerate, gentle). It is willing to yield to reason, full of compassion and good fruits; it is wholehearted and straightforward, impartial and unfeigned (free from doubts, wavering and insincerity)"*. Wisdom is the principle key to a fruitful marriage, not giving in to doubt and unbelief, but living by faith and seeking the Spirit of God for understanding one another.

God wants to take us from faith to faith and glory to glory in our relationship in Him. We must take the limits off the Lord and trust in Him to work in the hard places that seem impossible.

# Chapter 9

# "Wisdom Wins
**Wisdom is the power of survival.**

James 1: 5-8 (AMP) says: *"If any of you is deficient in wisdom, let him ask of the giving God {who gives} to everyone liberally and ungrudgingly, without reproaching or faultfinding, and it will be given him. Only it must be in faith that he asks, with no wavering, not hesitating, not doubting. It is like the billowing surge out at sea that is blown hither and thither and tossed by the wind. For truly, let not such a person imagine that he will receive anything {he asks for} from the Lord. {For being as he is} a man of two minds (hesitating, dubious, irresolute), {he is} unstable and unreliable and uncertain about everything (he thinks, feels, decides).*

Wisdom will cause you to defeat the bad cycles and generational curses that have attacked your marriage. The Holy Spirit is in our lives so that He can teach us, lead us, and guide us into all truth. If married couples are not in harmony with the word of God, how can they win the battle of death in marriages? All around the world, it is God's wisdom that we take counsel of and His word, so we can be more than conquerors. The Holy

Spirit is the leader, and if he is the leader, then we should allow him to lead us in everything.

If your marriage is damaged and both spouses are hurting due to the affliction caused by either person, then I want to encourage you and to tell you God wants to heal your land. Your land can represent your personal life, your children, money and friendships and whatever concerns you have. He wants to heal you.

<u>Wisdom is a principle key.</u>

In all of life's problems, wisdom is principle in all things. The great philosopher, King Solomon, never prayed for riches during his time to become king. He asked for wisdom to help him as the leader of the Israelites. Solomon reigned using wisdom. Solomon used great wisdom when he built the temple for the Lord to dwell there. (1 Kings, Chapters 5 - 7.)

**I am an overcomer through the power of prayer.**

The level of importance of the Altar.

"Prayer unlocks the heart of the Father and opens the heavens. It's a "dynamic principle"- no prayer, no life flow, and no revelation"- Kim D. Sharpton

2 Chronicles 7:14: *"If my people, who are called by my name, shall humble themselves, pray, seek (crave, and require of necessity) my face*

*and turn from their wicked ways, then will I hear from heaven, forgive their sin, and heal their land."*

**"Prayer unlocks the heart of the Father."**

Only healthy, anointed marriages can last with the Holy Spirit's involvement. He cannot release His healing power inside your lives if you don't yield to His embrace to heal you. We must recognize the call to Israel here in this verse of scripture. First, the Lord tells Israel to humble themselves - humility is the first key to a blessed marriage. The state of mind must be in a humble position to receive whatever the Holy Spirit wants to do in it. Second, the Lord tells Israel to pray. The second key is prayer and intercession. Prayer is communication with the Father, and it works well with praise. When a married couple come together in a powerful agreement, then the enemy will be put to flight. Matthew 18:19 says: *"Again I tell you, whatever you forbid and declare to be improper and unlawful on earth, must be "what is already" (harmonized together, make a symphony together) about whatever (anything and everything) they may ask, it will come to pass and be done for them by My Father in heaven".*

The third request to Israel from the Lord is to turn from their wicked ways. The Lord knows what wicked ways are there, and everyone has a level of unpleasantness in their life. The third key is turning from the unpleasant ways in your life. Whatever does not please the Lord in your marriage, turn from it and turn to committing to please Him in making your marriage pleasant before him.

The fourth thing the Lord told Israel He would do is open His ears to hear their request after they followed in obedience. The keys are: humbleness, prayer, and turning in action of responding by his people in obedient ways. Then would come the forgiveness of their sin (their arguing ways, fights and adultery) and healing of their purposes, wounds, scars, pains and brokenness. He is the God that heals.

**I am an overcomer - Fasting releases the dwelling power of God.**

John 15: 4-7 (AMP) says: *"Dwell in me, and I will dwell in you. {Live in me, and I will live in you.} Just as no branch can bear fruit of itself without abiding in {being virtually united to} the true vine, neither can you bear fruit unless you abide in me. I am the True Vine; you are the branches. Whoever lives in me and I in him bears much {abundant} fruit. However, apart from Me {cut off from vital union with Christ} you can do nothing. If a person does not dwell in me, he is thrown out like a {broken-off} branch, and withers; such are gathered up and thrown into the fire, and they are burned. If you live in me {abide vitally united to Me} and My words remain in you and continue to live in your hearts, ask whatever you will, and it shall be done for you."*

When a couple fasts together, it strengthens the faith and trust they both have in God, and it intensifies the unity anointing which married couples have. Also, when two come together in sincerity and fast for overcoming power to overcome failure, it will take them into a greater place of surrendering to God. Actually, fasting will intensify the power of God in the marriage.

***I am an overcomer - Prayer releases the dwelling power of God.***

Prayer is one of the foundational riches into the kingdom which releases great manifestations of power. Ephesians 3:20 -21 speaks clearly concerning the power working within us; the invisible power of God seen through operative faith. Prayer and faith go hand in hand. It can't operate unless one believes. I am an overcomer because I trust and believe that the Lord is a rewarder of them that diligently seek him. Hebrews 11:6 o *"But without faith it is impossible to please Him, for he who comes to God must believe that He is, and that He is a rewarder of those who diligently seek Him".* As we continue to walk in undeniable faith, it will grant us access in areas that we could not otherwise get into. We could never unlock the supernatural power of God unless we believe.

<u>1 Kings 19: 5-8 - Elijah</u>

*"Then he lay down under the bush and fell asleep. All at once an angel touched him and said, "Get up and eat." He looked around, and there by his head was some bread baked over hot coals, and a jar of water. He ate and drank and then lay down again. The angel of the LORD came back a second time and touched him and said, "Get up and eat, for the journey is too much for you." So, he got up and ate and drank. Strengthened by that food, he traveled forty days and forty nights until he reached Horeb, the mountain of God".* In <u>1 Kings 19:5-8</u>, the story of Elijah speaks of supernatural provision, protection and power. First, we have an angelic

presence appearing to the prophet Elijah waking him up to prepare him to encounter a conquest. The conquest that he was going to encounter was going to showcase God's power before Jezebel and Ahab. Elijah had such a strong level of warfare. Elijah was confronted on Mount Carmel. He had to show them that his God is greater than theirs. This confrontation leaves him running for his life because he felt threatened of the fearful opposition he faced. He went to Beersheba in Judah (1Kings 19: verse 3). The Lord protected the life of his prophet.

As the story continues, the fear upon Elijah was so great until he hid from Jezebel fearing he was the only prophet left. There are circumstances we will have to confront in life that will leave us in fear. However, God does not want you to walk in fear, but in courage. The Lord allows situations to confront our lives, so He can showcase "His" power within us. Elijah is awakened by an angel who speaks to him and gives him direction, who shows Elijah who he is and the power that works within him.

**I am an overcomer in the Holy Ghost abiding love.**

Galatians 5:22-25 (AMP):

*"But the fruit of the {Holy} Spirit {the work which His presence will accomplish} is love, joy {gladness}, peace, patience {an even temper, forbearance}, kindness, goodness {benevolence}, faithfulness, gentleness {meekness, humility), self-control (self-restraint, continence}. Against such things there is no law {that can bring a change}. And those who belong to Christ Jesus {the Messiah} have crucified the flesh {the goodness human nature} with its passions and appetites and desires. If we live by the {Holy}*

*Spirit, let us also walk by the spirit. {If by the Holy Spirit "we have our life in God, let us go forward"* {walking in line.} Our conduct controlled by the spirit. As we abide in God as born-again believers, we must allow the fruit of the Spirit in our marriages to manifest.

Many times, in marriages, husbands and wives are in conflict due to the lack of self-restraint and not enough of spirituality. No one wants to walk in the fullness in the Spirit. The fruit of the Spirit is not alive in many homes. If I may use husbands as an example because they are the head in the Spirit and in the natural; this is God's divine order for families.

Family is divinely ordained by God. They were the first in creation. Adam and Eve were the first man and woman, and Cain and Abel were the first children to Adam and Eve. They were the first ordained to manifest as examples of healthy relationships among humanity in the earth. They were the first to experience the true love from the Spirit of God. So often, marriages fail due to this special emotion, Love. Love is about commitment and worship. It does not condone but it endures. True intimacy develops from this true love dynamic. True love is definitely a part of true worship. The fruit of love is a characteristic of the Spirit of God and it is a part of worship. When married couples show love, they are giving divine worship to God and pleasing Him. Let me explain - love is response to worship. When married couples are loving each other, they are telling God nothing will ever separate them from His love. In addition, when you love each other you are answering the call to true worship.

The Holy Spirit is a gentle spirit. He will only come into your relationships by request, and every born-again relationship should allow him in. As people allow Him to enter into their marriage, the relationship should flow smoothly. It is God's desire that His Spirit be allowed to empower marriages because of the vow of covenant made between man and woman.

"Shachac" is a Hebrew word which describes bowing and kissing; it speaks of close contact. Webster's dictionary gives a more detailed definition of the subject of worship: paying divine honor to God: a feeling of respect and reverence for power, position, merit, and virtue; dignity, worth, obsequious devotion and paying divine honor. Marriage is worship with God. It also describes how Christ feels about His church. It is true romance with God. True love from the fruit of the Holy Spirit releases great motivation, honor, respect and commitment toward one another and God. It is the will of the Father that husbands and wives flow together in true love and hope, fearing one another in humility. Walking in love also creates an environment which gives the Holy Spirit room to speak to the hearts when everything is going wrong. Without love, we cannot do anything. True love denotes the beauty of relationship in the Spirit of God's eyes, and it purifies the married couple's minds toward one another. Love will determine how much joy you will gain through the power of love and respect for one another.

### *Joy unspeakable and full of Glory. I am joyful.*

Pure joy which comes from the Spirit of God is supernatural and is only produced through the Holy Spirit. Joy produces growth in the emotions and the soul. The word "Joy" comes from the Greek word, "chara". Chara has two meanings. It can mean gladness or happiness. In similarity for this word is "chairo" which means rejoice. Webster's dictionary gives a similar definition to the Greek. It speaks of the intense happiness or great delight; that which gives rise to this emotion or on which the emotion centers around the outward expression of the emotions. Scripture teaches us in John 15:11, that Jesus said to his disciples, "These things I have spoken to you, that My joy may remain in you, and that your joy may be full". True joy begins with the filling of a spiritual void from emptiness, I would say from relationship. Relationship stems from being together or tied with something or someone. Oftentimes, pure joy branches from Jesus as he is the root of your life. My first experience of joy is when I gave my life fully over to the Lord at the age of twenty-one. My life before accepting Jesus as Lord of my life was empty. I had many bad experiences: man trouble, drugs, alcohol, children out of wedlock and more. Yet, when I gave my life over to the Lord and begin to abide in him and He in me, I begin to bear much fruit in my life. Jesus said in John 15:5, "I am the vine; you are the branches. He who abides in Me, and I in him, bears much fruit ". This fruit includes God's nature and character in us. God blesses us and gives us life freely to enjoy in him. I never knew love like Jesus' love, a love that speaks peace to every storm cloud in my joy and gives me joy unspeakable. You may be in a season where Satan has tried to destroy everything under the sun and cause you to not receive the promises of God. Let me be more clear, "Satan has tried to make you feel unworthy by creating your own personal hell by worrying and thinking about the things that might go wrong in your life; such as sudden failures and loss of job, child, and other things. Suddenly, Satan takes your focus by turning your psyche onto things you have no control over in life. The bible teaches us that Satan comes to sift us as wheat – Luke 22:31. God does not want your value system to be placed in comparison of what you hold dear and can't handle. However, God wants you to value bad times, for it is the worst times in your life that are causing seeds to grow that's been planted. Years of toiling, planting and planning is well worth the oil of Joy that God is releasing on the inside of you. The Spirit of the Lord says that those the LORD has rescued will return. They will enter Zion with singing; everlasting joy will crown their heads. Gladness and joy will overtake them, and sorrow and sighing will flee away. God's Joy will crown you with continual delight.

### *I am an overcomer by defeating impatience.*

Patience is one characteristic that the Holy Spirit uses to help grow the Christian believer in life. Patience is defined as the capacity to accept or tolerate delay, trouble, or suffering without getting angry or upset. (www.dictionary.com)

The fruit of patience comes from the vine of the Holy Spirit and is unique in its class – <u>Galatians 5: verse 22</u>. Patience is one character everyone has to grow into; it does not happen overnight. Patience is something that everyone learns. It develops through trial and error. Patience causes longsuffering, meaning you can suffer long without complaining. When a child of God's character is tested, it brings a conditioning to the mind, spirit, and soul. In patience, the believer experiences the strength and power of God. It is so magnificent when patience can have its perfect work in your life.

Patience is usually manifested through a trial when you are suffering, and in one of the hardest periods in your life. Everything is rough and you want to come out of it victoriously. You may be in the midst of one of the fieriest, hurting trials in your life and want to be brought out, but it seems like you are stuck in pain, hurt, and seclusion. You feel like you are all alone and it has brought much discomfort in your life.

As I reflect back on my life, I was in much need of patience. <u>Romans 12:12</u> says: *"Be joyful in hope, patient in affliction, faithful in prayer"*. I often was discomforted by problems in my life; trials that would process me and produce greatness. As time went on in my life, I saw that I needed to be really processed in learning, hoping and trusting. I had to understand that what was being done in my life was a much-needed process.

For those who are reading this book, I urge you to understand that patience is a much-needed process in your life. You may be that Pastor who's waiting for your ministry to grow and you've done everything from planting seeds in soil to over-turning soil, while waiting patiently for harvest. I want to encourage you not to get discomforted in your wait but allow the Father's process to work for your good. Those days of barrenness do not mean defeat or that your ministry is not going to grow. What it means is you are in a process. Processes take time, and sometimes it can be a process of weeding out before you can see growth or new harvest. Galatians 6:9: *"Let us not become weary in doing good, for at the "proper time" we will reap a harvest if we do not give up."* God does not want you to give up in the process. Although it may be long and hard, and sometimes unendurable. It will bring good in the end and the harvest will be greater than you can ever imagine.

# Chapter 10

# "Let Nothing Separate You from Loving One Another"

Oftentimes women say that they really would like to have their husbands love them, but other things or people are in the way of the love. Love will cause the husband and wife to avoid pitfalls and come into a light of victorious living. Once the veil of darkness is removed, then they can rejoice in the abundance of joy. It becomes sad and sickening when one allows a matter or person to come between their love. When you allow someone or something to come between your love, then you have allowed the love given to you from the Father to become absent, and that should not happen. Your love is the ingredient to form the true culture of value for one another. It's to manifest passion, physical affection and commitment. The covenant between the two is not to fall apart due to meaningless outside relationships that come to eat through the structure of your relationship, leaving it lifeless, broken, and ready for divorce.

<u>1 John 4:7-8 (KJV)</u>

**7) Beloved, let us love one another: for love is of God; and everyone that loveth is born of God, and knoweth God.**

*8) He that loveth not knoweth not God; for God is love.*

Also, when two come together in sincerity and fast, the overcoming power to overcome failure will take them into a greater place of surrendering to God. Actually, fasting would intensify the power of God in the marriage. The prayer of faith and praise will increase the level of compassion for one another and cause both to desire what God desires for them; which is life and prosperity for the marriage.

Romans 8:37-39

Let nothing separate you from Loving one another.

*"Yet amid all things, we are more than conquerors (and again a surpassing victory) through Him who loved us. For I am persuaded beyond doubt {am sure} that neither death, nor life, nor angels, nor principalities, nor things impending and threatening, nor things to come, nor powers, nor height nor depth, nor anything else in all creation will be able to separate us from the love of God which is in Christ Jesus our Lord."*

My marriage wasn't perfect. I can recall the first separation; it was six months into the marriage. We were having hard times. We could not see eye to eye for anything. Arguments seemed to happen on a daily basis. I could not understand why we couldn't get along. I wanted so much to know why our communication lines were down, and he had put up walls. He could talk to everyone but me. I wanted to know his deepest longings, and what pained him. The only thing he said was, "I don't think this marriage is going to work." I asked him, "Since it is so early in the marriage, can we go to marriage counseling?" He said, "No." He didn't think counseling would help. This was not clear to me and at that point, I was puzzled. This was my spiritual head and covering. Does he hear from God? Why is he leaving me? My husband made so many excuses not to want to be home. At this point, everyone was in our marriage - family, exes and other people. His language was very negative concerning family. It was his way or no way. I was hurt and in utter disgust.

Then, there was a particular woman who I had questions about. "Why is this woman around? Is it important that her presence be around so much? Does she have a significant other?" She was always at my home. Her excuse was she wanted to see her children. Every time I turned around, she was at the church we attended and following us to his preaching engagements. So, the next excuse was she was picking up our son.

Our problems grew from there, and things went downhill. I was fit to be tied. I was considered to be a villain in my marriage because I wanted answers to my questions. But, there was always an abusive response to my questions. This is sad to say, but I was starting to feel like I was on the back burner of the relationship. As time persisted, finally he came back; but with a chip on his shoulder and demands of what he was not going to do. His statements were, "I am the head of the home and what I say goes." I said to him, "What about me, do I have any say in the matter?" He said, "No." His remark was, "Just be quiet, just say nothing. You can sit, smile, or grin. Just don't open your mouth." This level of control was unbearable; he wanted to control my words, actions and deeds. The word "Control" means, to exercise authority and influence over. He wanted to have authority and influence over my will. This act of control was dangerous. I felt that I was in a prison. I couldn't voice my opinion.

The abusive ways increased. He began to take his anger out on the children. Every little thing was me and my children's fault. I became angry because I was limited in the home. My voice was silenced. All I could hear was his abusive statements against me; and what I was or wasn't in his eyes. My children could not measure up to his standards; they were just "bad kids." He never spoke to their potential or future as blessed. All he could say was, "They are going to be jail birds and early parents."

Word power and word abuse is an epidemic in society today. Only if we were mindful of the power of words we speak, we could change lives and situations.

<u>Deuteronomy 30: verse 14</u> --

*"The word is very nigh unto thee, in thy mouth, and in thy heart, that thou mayest do it."*

When we take into account that words can release us to great promises, the word is nigh us to heal the broken areas in our lives and to bring great turnarounds. The Father loves us so much that He longs for our personal and family healing. It does not matter what is presented; what matters is that our heart is not entangled with a yoke which will limit our possibilities in life. God's love is so gracious; He wants us to encounter gracious words which will present wholeness.

Proverbs 16:24 –

"Gracious words are a honeycomb, sweet to the soul and healing to the bones."

In this verse, King Solomon deals with the level of speech - what we say and how it's said, that will bring healing to one's life. Words that comfort and build up to edify a foundation of life is sweet to the soul and bones of man. They cause the emotions to lay on the sweetness of the Master's loving touch through the power of His words. I want to warn those who speak harshly, and do not allow the Holy Spirit to use your mouth to speak words that will bring wholeness and healing. This will only bring turmoil into the lives you speak into.

    I want to encourage those who feel caged-in like a bird with a broken spirit, due to harsh words spoken over your life, which have left you wounded and unable to conquer in life. It seems like those words you heard have come to decorate your life with patterns of hurt, pain, and confusion. I want you to know that the Father transitioned your life to win. The Lord has sweetness for your spirit which will release healing and stability. This hurt from words has just been a process which will take you into the weight of the Father's Glory and His divine presence. Allow what has been a shadow of negativity, take you into sweetness with the Father every day. You will find that the words which have come to limit your mindset from growing and your spirit from healing, will be a memory that will fade away, as the Father heals.

# Chapter 11

# *The Dynamics of Negative Words on Children*

Being a parent is not about control. Our use of words to keep children in their place has to be changed. Our words could be used to build up, to help and to provide our children with lifelong tools for them. Our love, with encouragement and liberating words, would mean they will never doubt themselves, or take a double look in the mirror to think whether they like themselves or not.

Many have been recipients of name calling, verbal words of undermining, and disrespect as a child. Or worse yet, verbal abuse, in the past that has not been resolved, unfortunately carries through to adulthood; impacting their present and informing their future. The abuse resonates and poisons the self-worth and esteem. It can dictate how we treat others and how we view the world.

Each nasty, destructive word is carved in the insides of a person. It weaves itself into one's thoughts, breath, hopes, and dreams. Its toxic remnants seep insidiously through the veins and melds with one's DNA. Words wielded destructively can deconstruct and negatively reconstruct the human psyche with dire consequences. Why is it that it's an acceptable practice to call our young ones Brats, Rascals, Little Buggers, Monsters or simply Nuisances? Why is it that we would be furious if someone called us one of these? Yet, we use this terminology for our own children. Why is it that we are outraged if they are called names on the schoolyard, but from the time they are in the womb, it's common practice to call them everything from munchkins to Little Turnip. How is this affecting our children, and what is the message of self-worth we are sending out to them?

Each negative word you use becomes a deadly weapon of warfare. In other words, you yourself, are your own enemy. Negativity eats away at your potential and chips away at your dreams and ambitions, leaving one hopeless with no energy to move into vision. Your life can be affected by negative words and behavior, choking the very vitality of life from you. The words, like self-hypnosis, leave you ineffective, heavy and gray on the inside.

Your Psyche may be marked and effected, leaving you to feel stupid, worthless, ugly and idiotic. Subconsciously, you begin to believe what is said over your life and come to believe the negative words that haunt your life and hang over your soul.

Satan's declaration over your life is not true. It is a lie! You are what the Heavenly Father says you are. This day, you must know that your life is so very important; and what has been declared over your past shall not make its way into your new beginning! Hope is yours and it is waiting on you to grab hold to it. The wholesome words of our Lord Jesus are "health to the bones." They are the means of curing the diseases of the mind; and of healing wounded spirits, broken hearts, and broken bones. They make the bones which were broken to rejoice. Whatever heals the bones, strengthens the whole man. A man's strength lies much in his bones. These wholesome words strengthen the inward man, and cause believers to go from strength to strength, to hold on, and to persevere to the end.

<u>Proverbs 12: verse 18</u> say *"The words of the reckless pierce like swords. But the tongue of the wise bring healing."* God is saying the use of negative words will cut, and hurt, and bring wounds. Reckless words that are intentionally used to destroy people, are like taking a knife and stabbing them in the heart. If ever you encounter this type of emotional turmoil in your personal life, let your tongue be wise and bring health. It is an awesome thing when you can use your tongue to bring "healing" and "life" to a situation.

*"Therefore, submit to God; resist the devil and he will take flight."* —<u>James 4: verse 7</u>. Let's pray for those who are suffering due to negative words spoken over them and their children's lives.

*"Father, in Jesus' name, I take authority over the power of negative words, in Jesus' name. I break the power of negative words spoken against my destiny and my offspring in Jesus' name. I declare and agree that every curse is broken by the power of Jesus' blood and I speak blessings the lives*

*of those and their offspring who are going through the power of negative words, in Jesus Christ's name. Amen"*

### **Children are seeds of greatness.**

Always, I say I live in abundant life changing circumstances. We are blessed and not cursed, and we are the promised seed. Overturn Satan's declaration against your home. Speak the purpose and will of God over you and your children. Always speak this: *"My children will excel in all things, at all times, with all people."* Declare and decree that they are God's kingdom children; and God's kingdom will come, and God's will shall be done. Declare and decree that your children are more than conquerors.

Declare and decree your child will walk in kingdom favor. He or she "will" possess all that God has for them. I declare and decree the demonic prophecy over their lives "will" be broken. Prison will "not" have them, but they will be blessed beyond measure. Remember, your tongue is an active force. With it, we can change the course of life.

This type of abusive treatment has continued down through the years. As we read Genesis, Adam didn't abuse Eve or the animals that God gave him authority over. He took care of them. Man has a great responsibility to provide financially. He is to make his family feel safe and secure. He is to love them and bring hope to them. He is not to fist beat them, verbally abuse them, mentally abuse them or emotionally abuse them. Husbands are to wash their wives with the Word of God (see – Ephesians 5:26). I couldn't understand why my husband did not love me like I loved him. The fact that he didn't was evident by the abuse he was showing me and my children.

Fathers are to be governors over the home. The destiny of the child lies in the power of the Father. Children are the balance within the family structure; they are gifts from the King. This is the reason why God called the woman to be productive in the family. The lineage lies with the woman. The bible says, that children are our reward. <u>Psalm 127: verse 3</u> says, *"Lo, children are a heritage of the Lord; and the fruit of the womb is His reward".*

Children were given to us to bless our lives, and to add to our generations. They are a great assignment from our King, and yes, without them our generation would not be abundant.

1 <u>Samuel 1: verses 9-11</u>, brings the account of Hannah: Hannah, beloved by Elkanah, was barren and wanted a son very much. She cried in her heart with desire to bring forth. She didn't have any legacy until her son came forth. The bible teaches that she went into the tabernacle and cried before the Lord, earnestly, until he granted her request. The key point in this story is the promise which Hannah made to God. The bible says she vowed to give her son over to the Lord all the days of his life. What did Hannah do? She surrendered her privilege of raising her son. She dedicated him to the Lord. This parent dedicated the child to the creator. It is a duty of a born-again parent to give their children back to God; for God

has need of all children. They are to be used as instruments for the kingdom of God.

Let's take a look at Samuel, Hannah's son. After being weaned from his mother, he was placed under Eli the priest's supervision to minister in the tabernacle all the days of his life. - <u>1 Samuel 1: verse 28.</u>

Let's look at the greatness of Samuel; he was a special child. His name means, "Asked of God", signifying his mother's request for him. Samuel's lineage was so important because he was a descendent of Levi. His bloodline was of the priestly line. To review Samuel's ministry - he served as prophet, priest, and judge of Israel. Samuel was used greatly by the Lord and those around him saw him as a man of God. He lived a life of dedication and was well loved by the Lord. As parents, it is ordained by God that we shape and train our children to "Love" the Lord. Samuel was a child prophet. Hannah didn't speak ill of her son, and neither did she curse his destiny. She turned him over to the Lord.

What is this telling us as parents? Our children are blessed and highly favored of the Lord; He treasures a child. What God sees with a child is an open willingness to be used. So, it is very imperative that we understand that children are our future and we are responsible for shaping their destinies until they are old enough to understand their purpose in life. We are to train them up in the way they should go. (Proverbs 22:6).

Before I got married, I trained my children how to love the Lord. When I would go to prayer, they went too. I would lay them on the altar and anoint them and ask God to have His way in their lives. It was hard as a young woman raising three children alone, but God heard me. When I asked for a mate to help me, little did I know the one who would come would be the opposite of what I asked for? It was hard for me to understand his purpose to abuse. It was very important that he could see my children's destinies like I did. He, as the head of the home, was to be held totally responsible for training them in righteousness. Training goes deeper than spankings. Simply training can be just living a life of righteousness before them. A child remembers what is before them and how they are being treated.

For instance, a problem broke out at my home and my daughter was small, about seven years old. She was eating at the table, and she was full and didn't want to finish her food. My husband told her to finish her food. When she replied, she was full and could not eat any more, she began to puke her food up. He put her face down into her vomit and made her eat it. This event never left her mind. As a parent, I felt defeated because I was not there to keep this type of abuse from happening to my daughter.

The influence that he had over my children was ungodly and such behavior should not have been in our home. My daughter began to look at me as her enemy, and not her friend, because her safety zone was violated by a man called Daddy. Children look to their parents as heroes, and as the best people in the world who have their best interest at heart. I was scared. I didn't know how I was going to gain her trust again. I tried everything to bring healing, but she rebelled.

The door was opened for more unhappiness because after that event, my family was torn apart. My home was under a strong demonic attack. I was broken-hearted, bitter, and angry because my child was hurt in the worst way. I wept continually and talked to the Lord about this, trying to make sense of this problem. No excuse could be thought of for what happened. I couldn't't talk any more to my husband. I tried begging him to understand that his way of training children was unrighteous. I was apologetic of the marriage and the negative consequences due to poor parenting skills.

I didn't know how to approach this problem in my home; the devil had it and this was a critical moment for my family. The principles of the word of God were ignored and my household was suffering. I was still for a moment! A fragmented woman suffering in silence! There was no one I could talk too about this abuse we suffered.

<u>1 Samuel 1:9-11</u>: Hannah was a woman of integrity, commitment, and faith. She suffered in silence. As we take account of the scriptures, Peninnah provoked Hannah. Peninnah taunted Hannah because she could not give birth. As I read, Hannah's character was humble. She was a quiet soul. She did not try to revenge herself; but she was tired, angry, and bitter in her soul. The bible didn't record that she confronted Elkanah about his other wife. She just wept bitterly in silence before the Lord. She had no

strength to fight. This woman became passive to her circumstance, which was critical. All Hannah had was a silent cry.

Sometimes when critical problems occur within the home, women conceal the matters, as opposed to dealing with them; especially when it involves sensitive matters like this. I was ashamed, and I didn't know who to turn to. Every time I would think of what he did, I wanted revenge. I wanted to get him back for my child. She was angry, and I didn't know how to express forgiveness to her. She went through a trial that was going to affect her entire life. Children deal with circumstances differently than adults do.

# Chapter 12

# "Console and Protect"

Isaiah 40:1-2 – *"Comfort, yes, comfort my people, says your God. Speak comfort to Jerusalem and cry to her that her warfare is ended, that her iniquity is pardoned; for she has received from the Lord's hand double for all her sins."*

Let me explain this passage in Isaiah 40:1-2. The Lord sent His prophet to speak comfort to His people Israel. They had just come out of captivity as a result of their sins. Despite their hard trial, He was concerned about them, as He is concerned about you. Your trial may be your marriage, your children, or your work place. The Holy Spirit does not leave anyone comfortless. God sends anointed, appointed people to speak into your lives with comfort and peace. You may not understand why the trials you are going through are so heavy; but it is because God wants to get the best out of you. "He" not only comforts, but "He" provides protection – it is the Master's call to protect us even when we feel defenseless. He is there all the time to defend and fight every battle that comes upon us. As a parent, I felt like I didn't do everything in my human power to protect my daughter; but her cry didn't go unnoticed. Psalms 24 says, "The *earth is the Lord's and all its fullness; the world and who dwell therein; the world and those who dwell therein. For he has founded it upon the seas, and established it upon the waters. Who may ascend into the hill of the Lord or who may stand in His holy place? He who has clean hands and a pure heart, who has not lifted up his soul to an idol, nor sworn deceitfully. He shall receive the blessing from the Lord and Righteousness from the God of his salvation. This is the generation of those who seek him, that seek your face, O Jacob. Selah*

*Lift up your heads, O you gates! And be lifted up, you everlasting doors! And the King of Glory shall come in.*

*Who is this King of Glory?*
*The Lord strong and mighty,*
*The Lord mighty and battle.*
*Lift up your heads, O you gates! And lift them up, you everlasting doors! And the King of glory shall come in.*
*Who is this King of glory?*
*The Lord of host,*
*He is the King of Glory. Selah"*

This Psalm is recognized as a conquering Psalm. It encourages God's people of His deity and serves to fight the battle in the mind. When there is much trauma and pain in your life, the enemy will use the trauma and pain to flood your mind with negative thoughts. The mind is delicate, and it needs to be renewed "daily". Despite the thoughts in my mind, I had to overcome evil thoughts with good deeds.

Since we both were leaders in the church, taking this matter before the Pastor was the best thing to do at this point. This matter was an emergency. The following Sunday after church service, I told the Pastor what my husband did. The Pastor was appalled by his minister's actions in the home. He couldn't understand that he had a minister under him with a cruel nature toward children. Pastor dealt with it and sat my husband down; and would not allow him to preach for a long time until our family was restored and healed. I can be honest; I was fearful in my home. My mind was clouded with thoughts of doubt and revenge.

For those who may be in the center of a situation like this:

*First* - Take counsel of "the Lord". Seek Him on what to do concerning the problems that arise in your life. Then, pray that revelation and guidance lighten your paths.

Let's pray for divine direction and instruction to lighten your path.

Prayer of forgiveness:

*"Father, in the name of Jesus, I pray for the heart and condition of the soul for deliverance, guidance and healing. I pray for repentance in Jesus' name, and forgive us for holding on to thoughts of revenge, doubt, dislike, and anger. Cleanse us, Your people, from holding on to the past*

*and help us to thrust forward into the future. Amen"* I decree and agree for your divine healing in the heart, mind and soul.

## No time for lame excuses

Webster's dictionary gives a clear meaning of a "lame" excuse - weak and ineffectual; unsatisfactory. Some of the excuses we come up with are ineffectual. Let's look at Adam.

Adam was the first man. God thought of him and created him from the dust of the earth. Let's take account of what the Lord said, *"Let us make man in our image after our likeness"* - <u>Genesis 1:26</u>. The Father created man and equipped him with power to subdue and execute authority over every living thing on the earth. Can you imagine having power over everything in the earth, every living thing -- the fish, the land, and vegetation? God made him the chief ruler over the earth. The only thing he was instructed to do was not eat of the tree of the knowledge of good and evil. (Genesis 2: 16, 17) Adam had it good. He was ruler over the earth with great responsibilities to name the fish and the livestock, and to till the ground. Adam had great favor that could someday cause him to live forever. It was the Father's design for him to be in a great place to receive a crown of life. Adam grew lonely, weary, and tired. He wanted companionship, and God saw the need and honored him.

The second chapter of Genesis tells of the design of Eve and how God put Adam to sleep, took a rib from Adam, and made his jewel. Adam took one look at her and called her "woman" and said, "She is flesh of my flesh and bone of my bone. She shall be called woman because she was taken out of man." It was God's determination to make Adam a suitable mate. Eve was suitable for him. She was designed to help meet his mental, emotional, spiritual, social, and physical needs. God showed his son what it was like to have a real woman by his side when he created Eve. Adam's reality of having a real woman by his side to help him in the earth, was more than a notion. Adam's lonely days became his happy days and his void was filled. When it seemed like everything was purposeful for life, flourishment was everywhere. He had dominion over the earth and a beautiful wife; and was happy, with no sorrow at all.

Remote changes came into Adam's life. The tempter came to tempt Eve. The determination of Satan was to cause man to fall into sin and cause them to lose position with God. That is what happened. Afterwards, when Adam heard God walking in the Garden, he was afraid. Fear sat in because he didn't know what to do. When God confronted the situation of disobedience, Adam said, "It was the woman you gave me." What a lame excuse Adam gave his Father. Many of us can come up with thousands upon thousands of lame excuses, but none of them will line up to the obedience required. Excuses will cause God to dismiss some blessings out of our lives. A lame excuse only comes when you have done something wrong, when it should have been done right. It is nothing but unsatisfactory actions that could be stopped if only one would "Listen" unto the voice of God.

How to hear God's voice and obey it – The voice of God: <u>Deuteronomy 28: 1 –2</u>*"If you fully obey the LORD your God and carefully follow all his commands I give you today, the LORD your God will set you on high above all the nations on earth."*

The Lord set foundational truths for the child of God who will be willing to obey and listen to His voice. In having a good relationship established with the Master, one must be willing to express "listening" to His heart. As the Father's heart beats with a passion for His people to hear what He has to say, it becomes so imperative for them to obey. Oftentimes, we mislead ourselves by not listening or hearing correctly.

My home was torn apart due to the temptation provided by the devil and the lack of obedience. When the Lord speaks, what excuse should be provided? None. If only people would listen to the Lord, unnecessary suffering could be eliminated from our lives. Sometimes suffering helps bring Glory out of your life. It also helps to break you and bring you into alignment to the word of God. After Adam's sin was exposed, God had to evict him from the garden. This is what sin will do. It will terminate your blessings and promises that were supposed to manifest in your life. Excuses often will bring a broken bridge between God and you. It will cause a level of broken trust and unworthiness between you and God. God will now lessen His trust of you because of the excuse made to Him.

The action in my home was a priority to be taken care of. I told the Lord and went to our Pastor at the time, and the matter was handled. No one has the right to be abused - be it mental, verbal or physical.

Children are special to the Lord. Luke 18:16 says, *"But Jesus called them unto him, and said, suffer little children to come unto me, and forbid them not: for of such is the kingdom of God."*

As a parent of three children, I do understand the attack of the enemy when he uses the child or children to bring more stress than usual. It was hard raising my three children with my step-children, because my husband's child-rearing was different than mine. He saw things out of a negative eye, opposite to seeing and speaking the Word of God over all the children. Despite what we as parents go through, it is our job to love the children and to provide "just" treatment, love and compassion as God–fearing parents.

# Chapter 13

# "She's A Jewel"

*"Then those who feared the Lord spoke to one another, and the Lord listened and heard them; so, a book of remembrance was written before Him for those who fear the Lord and who meditate on His name. "They shall be mine," says the Lord of hosts, "On the day that I make them my jewels. And I will spare them as a man spares his own son who serves him.* Malachi 3:16-17 MSG .

    The beauty of a woman lives within her essence, within her internal character. A good woman is one who fears the Lord. She is joyful, kind, loving, and nurturing. Whether such a woman is a believer or an unbeliever, she is equally important to the Lord. It does not matter. Proverbs 31 gives a great description of a beautiful jewel, but also a wise woman. The Proverbs 31 woman was what you would call a woman of great faith. She stood the test of time and understood what was needed to guide a home in the early Jewish century, as it would also be needed for today's faith. Proverbs 31:26-29, gives a clear description of a jewel that many may call a woman of virtue.

*26 She opens her mouth with wisdom, and on her tongue [is] the law of kindness.*

*27 She watches over the ways of her household and does not eat the bread of idleness.*

*28 Her children rise up and call her blessed; her husband also, and he praises her:*

*29 "Many daughters have done well, but you excel them all."*

The virtuous woman was a woman of excellent value and price. She understood what it was to lead her family in faith. She served the Lord with diligence; she didn't eat the bread of idleness. The virtuous woman was not lazy; she did chores around the house. Sometimes women get so busy until they forget their home, especially if they are career women. The Proverbs 31 woman did not neglect her family. She took her position as a wife and mother seriously. She worked tirelessly to make her family feel comfortable. She was a God-chaser. She sought after God with her whole heart, mind, and soul. She was kind-hearted. She understood giving. She gave to the poor.

The virtuous woman in Proverb 31 did not have a name recorded, but the bible recognized her as virtuous, and one of strength, efficiency, and ability. One of strength of character, that is moral strength and firmness. This means she was built to do what she did. In this chapter, I want to minister to the women of God who feel they can't measure up to the virtuous woman. You are molded, handcrafted, and designed by the Father, in strength and efficiency to build your home and lives. Ladies, you are bad (awesome) in the Holy Spirit. You are blessed because you trust in Him.

You are blessed because your strength is locked in the Lord. You are blessed because you walk in the way of the Lord. You are blessed as you keep his testimonies. You are blessed as you seek the Lord with your whole heart. You are blessed as you fear the Lord. Never feel that you are not good enough or measure your strength by another woman's. Every woman does not have the same ability or gift, but all of us are precious in the sight of the Lord; and we are a gift to every man that meets us because we are helpers to them.

Let's pray to understand our worth and value as a woman.

"Father, in the name of Jesus, I thank you that I am fearfully and wonderfully made. I am the righteousness of Christ; a Godly woman. Blessed and highly favored. I thank you Father, for I am a by-product of you. Father, I put you first in all my relationships be it marriage, family, and children. My heart is devoted to You; therefore, my foot shall not be moved. I declare the decree that my life is crowned with years and I shall see the goodness of the Lord in the land of the living. I declare and decree that I am shielded with wisdom, and charm and beauty are my armor. I declare I am a valuable gift. I am full of strength, ability, and character. I walk in love, kindness, mercy, and truth. My hands are not idle. My tongue speaks aloud good things and words of life. I shall have what I say because it lines up with Your words. Therefore, I am blessed because my testimonies are sure. Amen"

"She is the one God brings to you, to help bring out your potential man. She is the one who will help give you favor with the Lord. She is the *one that will come between you and the Lord when he gets angry with you for your lack of obedience. She will love you and have compassion when no one else will. Beauty in a person is never how they appear; it is how they act."* (Catherine Pulsifer)

Let's see <u>Exodus 4:25 and 26.</u> Moses was supposed to circumcise his son. It was the Jewish custom that all male children in Israel get circumcised, and Moses hadn't circumcised him right then. [Genesis 17: verses 12 -14] God was angry with Moses because he was disobedient. The bible says, Zipporah took a knife and cut off the foreskin of the penis of their son. Zipporah came between God and Moses. Actually, she became Moses' intercessor at the time. God was very angry because he did not obey. All sons were to be circumcised. It was the Abrahamic covenant. Therefore, because of the intervention of Zipporah, Moses was spared; God had mercy upon him. Sometimes in marriage, we forget how precious we are to one another. It is the small things we forget that grant mercy. If Zipporah wasn't there, Moses would not have been able to finish his task. She was so very important for the assignment. We must understand we need one another in order to survive. She brought the best out in Moses. She was his eyes. She took protective measures over her husband and her family. She acted in a state of heroism. She covered him. Moses' destiny would have been over because of his mindset of disobedience.

How many spiritual Zipporahs are ready to execute heroism for their families? It took a woman of sensitivity and instinct to know the move of God for her family. She told God, "No don't kill my husband because he has purpose and has to fulfill the mandate you have given him." It is time to take charge and stand in the gap. What she did was stand in the gap on behalf of Moses. She stood up and took authority.

Woman, it is time to rise to the occasion and call for mercy on the behalf of your brother, your sister, your friend and even your husband. He might not be in the right place with God, but God will honor "you", if you are in the right place. He respects righteousness. Zipporah was righteous in her actions and deeds. She was a jewel from God. No matter what the circumstance is, please God in your actions, deeds and motives. Understand that you are holding someone's purpose and destiny in your hands.

One day a sister I knew called me on the phone (her husband was very rebellious in the church and God continually asked him to do something in his marriage concerning his wife, and he would not obey). She asked me to pray for her husband. While in prayer, I began to cry and intercede, weeping on the behalf of her spouse. I was asking God for mercy for him. At that moment, I had his destiny in my hands. I took authority over the situation and came between the anger of God and him; he is still living today.

Just imagine if I would have walked in resentment because of the way my husband was acting toward me? I would not have been an instrument for the Lord to use.

At all times, we must be available to be used by the Lord, despite someone's else's level of ignorance and disobedience - you just be available.

Webster's dictionary defines "available" to mean, able to be used at any given time. No matter the circumstance, you must be sure to allow the Holy Ghost to use you. He does not want you to waste your time in hostility, wondering if the one you are interceding for understands the purpose or not. It's your job to be positioned to shield your spouse.

**Prayer of intercession for obedience:**

"Father, in the precious name of Jesus Christ, I plead the blood of Jesus Christ over my family, children, husband, and grandchildren. I come to intercede for obedience on the behalf of Your children. That Your children follow Your will and commands in Jesus' name. Father, as Your servant, Samuel said in 1 Samuel 15:22, "Has the LORD as much delight in burnt offerings and sacrifices as in obeying the voice of the LORD? Behold, to obey is better than sacrifice, and to heed than the fat of rams." Therefore, Father, I set aside to worship You in all things, knowing to obey You is better than sacrifice. I know my purpose is to walk before You in all diligence and to obey You. To walk before You, draw me closer to You, that I may carry out Your will in Jesus' name. Amen"

# Chapter 14

# "Dynamics of Love"

Love has many characteristics which manifests in many ways. The bible speaks of divine love. In respect to agape, agape love is a term used often within the church arena. This type of love describes God's attitude towards His son Jesus Christ and his creation. The bible states in <u>John 3: verse 16:</u> *"For God so loved the world, that He gave His only begotten son, that whosoever believes on Him should not perish but have everlasting life".*

Agape love is a wide-open description of the nature of God. Love can be acknowledged by prompted actions. If we can reflect on His divine concern for humanity, we see that God saw the state of man (the widespread, diseased condition that would have determined death for us). However, once again, God was faithful and had mercy by sending Jesus to redeem us back to Himself. Love is a characteristic of affection. Agape also gives a description of faithfulness, loyalty, unselfishness, and longsuffering. Love is life. It should be in the character of every believer. In hard times, especially in relationships, love should manifest itself. Paul says love endures, it is patient and it is not jealous. It does not wish to deny another of what he or she has. Love praises not itself, is not superior, does not behave unseemly, is not self-centered, and does not provoke. On the other hand, love is good-natured. It does not have intentions to destroy a person's life. Love does not find joy in hurting people, rather it rejoices in the truth. It believes in all things and hopes in all things. Love rules over any of the supernatural gifts given to the church. That is why Paul states, out of all the spiritual gifts, it is best to have love. (1 Corinthians 13:4-7.) Love is unmeasurable and all of God's people should embrace love and walk in it. Paul also states that if a person does not walk in love towards his brethren or sister, he is like a sounding brass or a tinkling cymbal. In other words, he or she is like a loud instrument, just making noise. God does not want an ear-splitting church when it comes down to love; He wants us to manifest his nature towards one another. His love saved the world from obliteration.

"*Husbands, love your wives, just as Christ loved the church and gave himself for her.*" (Ephesians 5: verse 25) Husbands are not to use their spiritual authority in any other sense. We find today that men are abusing their authority in the home and in the church. Marriages are in a suffering state due to the lack of the husband's obedience to God as the spiritual head in the home. The Holy Spirit has less influence in marriages, because the spiritual head fails to invite him in to nourish and teach him how to be the head of the home. The Holy Spirit is a teacher. It is His responsibility to teach us in all things. When the people of God forsake asking for help, then the Holy Spirit is limited in helping us as a body of believers, in every area of our lives – he is a teacher.

The body of Christ is in a suffering state, partially due to the disobedience of husbands. <u>Ephesians 5: verses 20-25</u> says: *"Husbands, love your wives, just as Christ loved the church and gave himself for her to make her holy. Cleansing her by the washing with water through the word, and to present her to himself as a radiant church, without stain or wrinkle or any other blemish, but holy and blameless. In this same way, husbands ought to love their wives as their own bodies. He who loves his wife loves himself. After all, no one ever hated his own body, but he feeds and cares for it, just as Christ does the church—for we are members of his body. For this reason, a man will leave his father and mother and be united to his wife, and the two will become one flesh. This is a profound mystery—but I am talking about Christ and the church. However, each one of you also must love his wife as he loves himself, and the wife must respect her husband."*

Paul, the writer of the book of Ephesians, presents the church as the body of Christ, the invisible church of which Christ is the head. Paul uses the book of Ephesians as a symbolism to marriage. He uses the human relationship to show Christ's love for the church. Paul used Christ and the church as an example to show married people how Christ has an undying love for his bride. His love is so pure, rich, and deep, that He gave his life for His bride (the church). In this context, Love is used as a demonstration to married people; their love is to be pure, loyal, rich, and deep. He does not hate the church that He died for, but he says that He loves His body and would do anything to keep her. Despite the wrongdoings that we have done to the Lord, He loves us with an everlasting love. Christ used the church as an example of how a husband should love his wife. The mystery of it all is an in-depth and profound meaning of the love Christ demonstrates to the church. Christ was very communicative to His body about love. The meaning goes beyond the natural use between husband and wife, because His love reaches the eternal use of the soul. Christ ministered love to His body by giving His life for it. The sole example is of a husband who is to love beyond the natural endless extent. The degree of love is to bring expectation, reconciliation, agreement, and balance to a Christian home.

**Prayer of agreement for the Christian Home:**

*"Father in the Name of Jesus, I declare and agree that the Father will announce and promote me and lift me up in His grace. I declare and agree the voice of witchcraft and word curses that have been spoken over my household be silenced in Jesus' name. I declare and agree, according to James 1: verses 6-8, my family will unify in faith, doubting nothing, Satan is defeated and I command peace to come into my home. I declare and agree, according to James 1: verses 2-4, that my household will stand against all adversity in the midst of hardships in Jesus' name.*

*I declare and agree, according to Ephesians 6: verses 10-18, we have the full armor of God on tightly fitted, and that we will be strong in battle to fight against the devil. We have on the belt of truth fitted around our waist, the breastplate of righteousness in place, our feet in readiness that comes from the gospel of peace, and the shield of faith, with which you* can destroy all the fiery arrows of the evil one. Also, we have the helmet of salvation and the sword of the Spirit, which is the word of God, to destroy the works of the enemy.

I declare and agree, according to Psalm 27: verses 1-2, that my enemies will stumble and fall. I declare and agree with Psalms 56: verse 9, that the enemy will turn back in the day when I call upon the name of the Lord. In Jesus' name. Amen.

# Chapter 15

# *"Seasons of Change"*

"Bad experiences are meant to turn into victory and "<u>Victoriously, He Makes All Things New</u>" - Kim D. Sharpton!

The design of the Lord is so beautiful, like the harmony and thirst for a new season and day. Who can declare the Father's majestic power? He turns bad days into good days, winter into spring and spring into summer. Every season becomes a new day and a new beginning. You would never know how to push forward until you let the old go and walk into the new. Newness of life and starting over will give you hope in positive directions for your life.

In one stage of my life, I didn't know how to embrace my victory or new season. It seemed as though I had loved and lost, but I had to embrace loss as a teaching tool for victory. The outlook I had on my life was nothing less than regret, instead of hope and rejoicing. Change is the process which highlights your perspectives into a new beginning. I could never foresee my life blossoming into beautiful. I thought the metamorphosis would never take place. Each stage in my life was in backward mode instead of forward. You may be that someone who is in the same place I used to be in; and it seems like your life is struggling and falling into a big pit. Each day you strive to move forward. You can't because your past stares you in your face. In other words, you can't live your past down. As much as you want to let go and move forward, the pit gets deeper and deeper. In this challenge of life, while gaining momentum in the direction in the Lord, our Heavenly Father is never in the business of leaving us in the pit of pressures in this life. He renews us with promises in radiance, in wisdom, and in full power and goodness - Victoriously. When you hear the word "power", you picture war, with the concept of winning. The Father wants you to know what you have engaged in. The operation of war is over; your new season awaits you to walk in it Victoriously. I love the seasons of fall, winter, spring, and summer because each of them is symbolic to cycles in a person's life.

Let me begin with winter:

**Winter Season:**

Winter is the season in the natural when you experience the coldest air drop in climate. In nature, you will experience freezing temperatures, snowy blizzards, heavy hail and ice pellets, and rain and snow mixtures. Your days will be shorter and nights longer. So it is, as in the natural, the same in the spiritual. Winter is characterized by coldness, misery, barrenness, and even death. Nothing is growing in the winter because it's cold; and many experience discontentment due to what is going on with them in that season of time. In the winter climate of your life, or in the night season, you will experience heavier storms. These storms will depict your attitude and how you react to what the Lord is trying to do in the next season of your life.

In the winter season, loneliness and discontentment try to settle in. They come to try your flesh. This storm is called a "fleshly" storm, and it hinders the newness of life. The devil wants the saved single, the married who is departing out of a bad relationship, and the widow who's being healed from the death of a loved one, to be hindered by the manifestation of the flesh. The manifestations of the flesh are these, according to Galatians 5:19: Adultery, fornication, uncleanness, and lasciviousness. You may be the one in the night season who wants to be snuggled up with someone, while in your winter season. Your storm could be fornication, committing adultery, picking the wrong mate, or simply not being patient enough to wait on the Lord for newness of life. If this is you, the Lord wants to declare peace in this winter or night season you are experiencing, because He does not want you to miss out on victory.

Jeremiah 3: verses 21 -23 says, *"A cry is heard on the barren heights, the weeping and pleading of the people of Israel, because they have perverted their ways and have forgotten the LORD their God. "Return, faithless people; I will cure you of backsliding." "Yes, we will come to you, for you are the LORD our God. Surely the idolatrous commotion on the hills and mountains is a deception; surely in the LORD our God is the salvation of Israel."*

In your winter season, it's not a time to walk away from the Lord and to fulfill your evil desires which will carry you away from the Lord. Winter or night season is preparation, planning and process time to go into your next place with God. This cycle in your life seems the hardest, but really, it's the greatest because it prepares you for the next new beginning. The Lord's ultimate goal during your time in the winter night season is to purify you, and to take out of you what's not like Him and make you new. In this season, your victory is contingent on your obedience; and it will take you into your next stage and process in the making of newness.

In 1993, in the winter phase of my life, it was a time of loneliness. I tell this story to help those who struggle in their winter season. It was during the winter storm outside, but also, I was experiencing a winter storm in the spirit which manifested in the natural. I was lonely. I wanted to be married, and each time I looked outside my window, all I saw was ice and felt coldness. Often, I would express to the Lord I wanted to be married, and I told him to make haste because I wanted to be with someone in my life. It's normal to want to be with someone. As a matter of fact, it's God's designed plan for those who are single to have healthy desires to be married; but with the right one whom the Father has "ordained" for your life. Well, I would sit by my window watching the ice fall from the trees. Oh, it was so pretty to see. On the inside, I had an inward struggle. My flesh was in battle with my spirit and I wanted companionship. My winter season seemed to be harsh. No one could understand it. Everyone was getting married around me. It was torment, but I had to learn to die to my wants, desires, and cares. What the Lord wanted to do in me was to groom me for what He had for me. I could not wait. I wanted the Lord to make haste. So, I moved in haste, and it was a wrong decision to move outside of the Lord.

2 Corinthians 5:17 says, *"Therefore if any man be in Christ, he is a new creature: old things are passed away; behold, all things are become new".*

You would never be successful in the next season unless you allowed the Lord to kill off everything that's not like Him. Then, you can become that new creature He wants you to be in the next season.

**Prayer for winter season:**

*"Father, in Jesus' name, this is my prayer for those in their winter season; that You would allow the harsh coldness and barren days to pass by your sons and daughters. I pray Father that You would allow death to come to the things that will bring sin into the lives of Your people. In Jesus' name. Such manifestations of the flesh as spoken of in* Galatians 5:19 -21 *- fornication, adultery, uncleanness, lasciviousness, idolatry, witchcraft, hatred, variance, emulations, wrath, strife, seditions, heresies, envying, murders, drunkenness, reveling. Such elements of sin kill characters and personalities. Therefore, those who manifest in any of these fleshly manifestations named, will die spiritually if not dealt with and delivered. Father, I ask for healing for those who struggle in their flesh in Jesus' name. Lord, I stand in faith and authority as a blood-washed believer and take*

*authority over the will of every manifestation of the flesh. I render them inoperable and ineffective in Jesus' name. Now Father, I decree Isaiah 61 over the lives of your people and ask your freedom and liberty in Jesus Christ's name. Amen."*

## **Spring Season:**

Spring is a season of rebirth, rejuvenation, renewal, resurrection and regrowth. In this season, the climate of a person's life begins to shift from dead to rebirthing or new. If you are coming from the winter season into the spring season, then you are in a season of metamorphosis in your life. Your life is transitioning into beauty and your spiritual trees are about to bloom. The climate of your life is about to get warm and breakthroughs are about to happen for your life. This is your time to rebirth. This prefix of "re": means to do it again. To rebirth defines a spiritual enlightenment causing a person to lead a new life.

Let me further explain. When you are rebirthing in your spring season, you are giving birth to new things, New things are springing forth. The cycles become more phenomenal. In revival, everything begins to come alive again. Therefore, you are able to start afresh in a new beginning. Rebirth speaks of new growth, new heights and new levels. You are able to establish new hopes and new dreams. Your ability to flex and move in the season becomes extremely easy. Hallelujah! In the new season, you are also able to reform new boundaries and new mindsets; you also perceive differently.

***Jeremiah 29:11*** says: *"For I know the plans I have for you, declares the Lord, plans to prosper you and not to harm you, plans to give you hope and a future".*

As you think in this season on that, everything you might have failed at was just a stage for a new road in your life. It's not over; it's just the beginning.

When Jeremiah 29:11 was recorded, Israel was in one of the longest seasons in their life. It was winter. Everything was dying, and they were in captivity for 70 long years. The Lord had to convey to them that it was not over for them; that He loved them and had plans to prosper and bring them into a new season, with plans to prosper. When they came out of the winter season into the spring, the Lord declared over their life HOPE, PROSPERITY, and a BLESSED FUTURE - He was going to make all things NEW for His beloved people. In your spring season, the Holy Spirit will grace you to produce better relationships that will be productive for your life. The Lord pronounces hope, meaning that we are to never give up. Despite what was in the past winter season, your spring produces better fruit of hope.

***Jeremiah 33:3*** says, *"Call unto me, and I will answer you, and show you great and mighty things, which you know not".*

In the spring season is when the Father reveals His heart as you position yourself in prayer. Prayer" is the road map to revelation - call on the Lord, He "answers", and shows mighty things you know not of. This is how the Lord works in the spring season. In the spring season, the Father reveals the greatest harvest changes to come to your life.

**Prayer for the spring season:**

"Father in Jesus' name, I come to declare that the past will be forgotten according to Isaiah 43:19 and "I will spring forth into new things". Father, I walk into my new season with victory, knowing I am more than a conqueror through Jesus Christ my Lord. Father, thank you for breakthrough, for the breaking of a new day is here. I praise You for Your joy and peace. For, now I am to rebirth everything that has been lost and regain insight of restoration in a new beginning. In Jesus' name I pray, Amen.

## Summer Season:

The Summer season is when the Father's grace is seen full of harmony, perfection and contentment. In the summer, the days are longer, and the nights are shorter. Much happiness is seen in the summer. Many engagements, marriages, new births, and breakthroughs happen in the summer season. The climate of your summer season in your life resembles breakthrough. In the summer season is when you experience the breaking of a new day. You will begin to see the Father's hand in the midst of your situation even greater.

<u>Amos 8:1</u>: *"This is what the Sovereign Lord showed me: a basket of ripe (summer) fruit".*

In the summer season of your life, you may see the fruit of life become ripe. This means you are more pleasant in your character. Your personality begins to reflect more of Jesus Christ and the Glory of His presence is arisen upon you. You begin to taste of the goodness of the Lord in the land of the living. In preparation of your new beginning, the Lord ripens you to be better. He cleanses all bitterness, so you can experience sweetness within. So, as you move forward in your life to the next phase of meeting someone, he or she will see the sweetness in you, and not the bitterness. In your summer season of breakthrough, the Lord creates an atmosphere of contentment and rest. He wants you to enjoy this phase in your life, because contentment means you are stable and satisfied with you and with what is happening in your life. Oh, Glory to God!

<u>Song of Solomon 2:12</u>: *"Flowers appear on the earth; the season of singing has come; the cooing of doves is heard in our land."* Solomon, the writer of Song of Solomon, describes the beauty of the elements of the summer season - flowers, singing, and cooing of doves being heard in the land.

I wrote a song called Summer Joy

For as the summer winds blow moving through the phases and chapters of in my life.
 I hear the Lord say
Focus on me I want you to smile

For there is nothing more than showers of summer joy that will lighten your life.
Your pain. The hurt and rejection has only been a reflection of due seasons of summer joy.
Focus on me because I want to make you free
Shower you with strength to overtake your weakness
Shower you with comfort to overtake your pain
For I give you joy in the midst of sorrow
Joy in the midst of pain
For my joy is your strength
My joy is your laughter
My joy is your gladness
My joy is never lacking
 The Lord says, Focus on me I want you to smile
For I shower oil of joy in the middle of your sad times
So, lift up your head oh ye people
Lift up your head oh ye people
For my joy is not lacking
My joy is full of gladness
My joy is your laughter
My joy is your strength
Focus on me I want to make you smile
I want my glory to shine on you like the rays of the sun
My joy blows in the wind and lights your atmosphere
My joy is full of delight
My joy is passion
My joy is sweet and delightful for your soul

.

    This song expresses the relationship of God and his beloved people. In this song God speaks to His servants to "focus on me for I want you to smile." For there is nothing more than showers that will lighten your life. Joy comes in many ways and in every season in a person's life. This song is a reminder of the joy of a new season after the storms are over. For God is calling harmony and peace as breakthrough with joy.

I walk in my NEW season with harmony and contentment, ready for the Lord to do what he wants. As I glance through the eyes of hope and future, I welcome destiny, I long and wait for the Lord's loving voice to speak over my life with the Word of God as He makes my life NEW. God's divine matrix of true victory causes the elements of storms that rage, to cease. Every storm and raging wind that comes in your life is to elevate your faith and teach you who Jesus really is, in your life. The Summer season has tropical storms that bring high winds and sometimes hail, thundering, and lightning; but once the storm ceases, breakthrough comes! In such cases, you will see the sunrise as the clouds break to show the sunlight. In some instances, God provides His covenant rainbow in the sky like a ribbon, to remind His children of what he promised Noah. Our sweet Lamb of God never misses a word or fails to bring His word to pass. Although the summer season brings breakthrough, there are times in some people's lives when a storm may hit. It does not mean that you are not deemed for joy; it just means that God has to bring a level of faith in your life.

Luke 8:22-25: *"Now it came to pass on a certain day, that He went into a ship with His disciples; and He said unto them, Let us go over unto the other side of the lake. And they launched forth.*

*But as they sailed, He fell asleep: and there came down a storm of wind on the lake; and they were filled with water and were in jeopardy.*

*And they came to Him, and awoke him, saying, Master, Master, we perish. Then He arose and rebuked the wind and the raging of the water: and they ceased, and there was a calm.*

*And He said unto them, where is your faith? And they, being afraid wondered, saying one to another, what manner of man is this! For He commanded even the winds and water, and they obey Him.*

Let's understand this, storms may come in **every** season and cycle of life; but, in the storms of life, the ability to calm it is there. Storms are trials that Jesus allows for a purpose. In order for your making to become greater, you must weather the storm. Then your destiny will be clearer. In Luke 8:22-25, Jesus had to teach the disciples a faith lesson. In this lesson, he wanted them to recognize their ability to speak to the storm. Your maximized ability can never manifest to fulfillment, until you use it. Use your faith (and speak forth with authority). What troubled Jesus was the length of time he had spent teaching the disciples; and yet, they still didn't exercise the power and authority they had. Instead, they screamed in fear, saying to the Master, "We are in trouble and the boat is about to sink. Do you care if we drown?" Jesus rose up in His power and authority and spoke "peace" to the storm. The disciples were amazed that the weather obeyed who He was.

Jesus has empowered us with His word and supernatural power to speak to climate changes in our lives, and they shall be different. Let me prophesy to you about the tropical storm in your life. This storm you are faced with has not paralyzed your ability to speak change to it. It is just pushing you to a place to speak to it and change your climate. This is your season to take hold of faith and increase in power and authority. Jesus allows such summer storms to come into your life to prove you in victory. You never see your maximized potential until you are faced with trouble that grips your heart; and you have to stand firm and speak to it without buckling.

So, I speak to your new summer that's coming with Victory. I am not going to leave you with a hope that you will never be faced with tropical summer storms, because you will. But, the LORD will give you faith to go through it! Now, we have learned about the summer storms and the victory that comes behind it.

**Let's pray about the summer season:**

*"Father, in the name of Jesus Christ, I take authority over the storms that will come to hit my life in the Summer season. I bind the storms that will come as raging seas that will try to overtake my like and steal my peace in Jesus' name. I speak peace to every mind and command my mind to align to the Word of God in Jesus' name. And I command sweet oil of joy will come and overtake minds in Jesus' name. Amen"*

**Autumn Season:**

Autumn is what I call the "middle-age" season. As the season changes, the coloration of trees changes from green to orange, which is beautiful. In this season, you will experience the Father's Grace. Such

Grace marks changes in your life. You may experience climates which heighten the colors in your life. Each color in the Autumn signifies beauty and richness of a new beginning. Have you ever noticed that in the Autumn season, harvest really springs forth? New beginnings take root and a new level of blossoming is seen.

Often, this season causes you to hibernate. God establishes rest. In the rest season, He causes some things to lay settled, so when the season of ripening comes, you will be able to blossom into harvest. You can only walk into a new season of healing, miracles, love, and hope if your mind is ready for those vibrant changes to come forth. You will never, ever be able to move into new areas in your life until you change the language in your mind. Sometimes mindsets are still in the winter-barren season cycle, and still speaking a dead language that never beholds the power of life. In this season, you must write down what the Father speaks to you, for the new beginning, full of Joy and Love. In this season, your mindset will only envision new history as you allow the Holy Spirit to walk you into a glorious destiny.

Revelation 21:5:

*"And he who was seated on the throne said, "Behold, I am making all things new. Also, he said, "Write this down, for these words are trustworthy and true."*

Newness always identifies with trust. You will never be able to embrace what is for you until you allow God to speak "BEHOLD" into your season. God wants you to recognize the change in your challenge; how wondrous everything is and will be. This is the "trust-covenant" that is being made to you. Behold, I make all things NEW.

This is the evidence that the Father has changed your identity. When God says, "BEHOLD", you ought to get excited because a shift is about to take place, and wondrous things are about to happen. If you read and notice in Revelation 21:5, The Lord says, "Behold, 'I' make all things NEW." When we see "I AM" in scripture, it means the nature of God (all existing) is declaring and making things sure. His existence is beyond human imagination. In other words, He exists in making all things new. The Father is living and breathing in making all things new. Let's look at the word "make": It means to create, to put together, to produce, and to assemble. In the sense of direction of these words, I will use all of them to bring clarity in meaning. When the word "create" is seen, it often aligns with miracles in the making.

In Genesis 2:7, when God created man in His likeness and His image, He formed man from the dust of the earth. It was a miracle - nothing ever yet heard of or seen in the history of creation. It was a miracle! I call it a creative miracle because God took man from dust and made him. I AM made a man new from the earth. This is what our Heavenly Father wants to do for you; to create a new heart, create a new mind, create a will, and create a new love. I love the combination of the words, "all things". All things mean "everything" concerning you will be created to work for your good. Hallelujah! There are miracles established in the Autumn season that will carry you from Glory to Glory. (2 Corinthians 3:18)

Whenever, though, they turn to face God as Moses did, God removes the veil and there they are—face-to-face! They suddenly recognize that God is a living, personal presence, and not a piece of chiseled stone. When God is personally present as a living Spirit; that old, constricting legislation is recognized as obsolete. We're free of it! All of us! Nothing between us and God. Our faces shining with the brightness of his face. And so, we are transfigured much like the Messiah; our lives gradually becoming brighter and more beautiful, as God enters our lives and we become like Him.

Here in 2 Corinthians 3:18, Paul is dealing with the process of Glory moving from one phase to another in His divine presence and experiencing the new habitat of His glory. Dealing with the inner person feature, while reflecting on the inner and outer form which is presented to the Father, we must be made new in order to inhabit His glory. The heart must catch the new knowledge of our King. New revelation that will cause the glorious anointing to rest upon everything that concerns us, will rip in every direction taken in life - be it ministry, personal and spiritual.

**Prayer for the Autumn season:**

*"Father in Jesus' name I declare and decree that this season of change will be the season of Heightened miracles in Jesus' name. I pray for blessings to overtake as I walk into this season. Thank you, Father for newness, miracles, and restoration as I walk into my new season. In Jesus' name. Amen"*

There is a song that Donald Lawrence wrote and produced; called "Seasons". Here are a few phrases:

*"I feel seasons everywhere, and I feel blessings in the air. Those seeds that you've sown, you're going to come into your own. Seasons, walk into your season.*

*Those seeds that you've sown, it's time to come into your own, seasons.*

*I believe we're in a time when God's gonna bless the saints. Those who have stayed, those who have prayed. He's gonna fulfil the promise he made. For I heard the spirit say it's your time. The wait is over, walk into your season.*

*Those seeds that you've sown, you're gonna to come into your own. .*

*Walk into your seasons.*

*I know that you invested a lot, but the return has been slow. You throw your hands up and say I give up I just can't take it anymore. But I hear the spirit say that it's your time. The wait is over. Walk into your season oh oh oh.*

*You survived, the worst of time. God was always on your side. State your claim and write your name. Walk into this wealthy place.*

*I hear the Spirit say, that it's your time. The wait is over."*

Donald Lawrence said it really well. It's time to walk into your NEW season! Stop waiting for breakthrough - it is here!!

Walk into your season. God has released a grace that will heighten greater miracles into your life.

Walk into your new season, as HE makes all things New!

# Chapter 16

# "Victoriously He Makes All Things New"

Victory is the formula of success which brings positive achievement against the enemy before it fails. I would have never achieved victory while in battle had I lost my faith and gave up on God. I had to believe that I was victorious in my battle no matter how bleak it looked; whether I was going to win it or have to stay in the battle longer to learn from it.

Please let me explain what I am talking about, each battle you go into can be won or lost; howbeit, all battles you learn from whether you win it or lose it. When you lose a battle, the trial you never overcome becomes a learning tool, and you will have to repeat that trial over again until you win it or learn from it.

In the last chapter, I discussed seasons of change and what happens in a person's life to help gain victory. It's very important to remain faithful and not lose heart during painful situations, because reaction determines an outcome. When I was faced with my trials, no it did not feel good. I was hurting for long periods of time. My wounds were open, and I didn't care who ministered to me, or prophesied to me; there was no manifestation until I decided that I was going to be free, and walk into victory, and become victorious. I had to determine my coming out stage, and when I did, I was on the road to becoming whole. As the scripture states in 2 Timothy1-3, *"As a soldier in battle you must be strong in the grace of Jesus Christ and be faithful then you must endure hardness as a good soldier of Jesus Christ because no one in warfare entangles himself with the affairs of this life."*

In short, this is why fruition of my victories have come to realization, because I maintained a positive outlook. I did not entangle myself with the affairs of the world and I was faithful to God. Victory does not mean while the battle is hot, that you are perfect. No. I made bad decisions. Earlier on in the chapters I discussed a marriage that I was in, which tore my life and family apart. However, I learned while faced with adversity, that God was working on me and in me,

God does a work in you while the battle is going on. This I never understood before, but while I was in the heat of my battle often God would direct me on what do that would help my character to grow. In other words, God was working in me and bringing out the best me, when the worst wanted to come out. Have you ever experienced those heated moments when you want to say the wrong things, but it just would not come out? They're still enrooted in your mind, but God begins to convict your heart because of the wrong thoughts in your mind. I am so glad the Father loves me so much to teach me that growing in faith takes skill to win and that sometimes you're going mess up in this walk. However, as he calls us deeper in Him, he lets us know that He is working on us and in us. So, don't give up even in your weakest moments. Philippians 1:6 declares this, *"Being confident of this very thing, that He who has begun a good work in you will complete it until the day of Jesus Christ."* So, you can become victorious and can live victoriously as God completes the work He starts in you. As I began to worship and usher the presence of God in; the soothing part of my victory was watching God shift and change a chapter in my life.

Suddenly, it felt like setting a bird out of prison, with freedom and liberty to live a life without chaos. Free to begin again. As I bowed my heart to the Father and began to worship; the determining factor of victory open anew in me. The Lord awakens you when he is bringing you into a new beginning. I know for me my awakening was singing; and worship brought me into a horizon of victory.

The story of Jehoshaphat blessed me because at the time of my hardcore battle, my home was divided into two kingdoms. Let me share the story in short. Israel wanted a King and God did not want them to have one because he wanted to be their King. However, He gave them one because of their asking; and the King they asked for was wicked, unrighteous and evil. In short, he divided Israel and Judah and they become two Kingdoms. As we would read more of the story about King Saul and Israel, much happened after the time of King Saul's reign. Israel had great Kings that turned their hearts toward God to worship Him; and others who were evil and who led them astray. During King Jehosaphat's reign as King, he was a good king in character and heart. Jehosaphat was

a strong and wise man, and he turned Israel toward God to worship Him. He took away all the idols in the land that Israel was worshipping; while God began to call Israel to worship Him in a deep and personal way.

Worship brings us to a deep place of victory. However, the enemy does not stop his harassment against you; he continues to fight because he wants you to be defeated. Meanwhile, while Satan troubles your destiny, God wants you to sing your victory in preparation that you'll be victorious. The Father always births a melody out of you while you are in troubled times, or it's a signature that you have won your battle. God is so strategic that He will never allow you to be overthrown in a battle if you put him first.

Jehosaphat and Israel assembled inside the Temple to pray before God. Jehosaphat saw the multitude of the people coming against them and knew the size of them was greater than his army. But hear what King Jehosaphat said to God, "Our eyes are on you."

God gathered His people in preparation, and Judah went first with singing, worship, and praise. This was God's signature that He's going first to defeat your adversaries.

In other words, our weapon is worship and praise. I am not going to look at what's in front of us; we are standing still to see your salvation. Through worship and prayer, I began to grow as a result in becoming victorious, in the likeness of God - in character, deeds, and action. I had to align to the divine purpose like King Jehosaphat did; and understand who was making me victorious.

This activation started with me putting God first, walking in obedience, living to worship, and praying until something happened.

### Sing of your victory

Perseverance births out newness. While I was in battle, God sent me before the enemy with a song of worship. I began to sing a new song of deliverance in the face of my enemy. These lyrics came to me and I began to write this song: Don't underestimate my power and my worship that dwells within me.

*"Deep calls to deep*

*Behold, the eye of the Lord is on those who fear Him, on those who hope for His lovingkindness, to deliver their soul from the weak places.*

*Deep calls unto deep*

*Truly God is omniscient, omnipresent, and omnipotent. He desires that we come to know Him in the splendor of His majesty, so we can worship Him freely and victoriously.*

*Deeps calls unto deep.*

*He assures, and He fulfills His promises. Yes, He does know our every need*

*Deep calls unto deep*

*Repeat: Come says the spirit of grace in to my deep place of glory for I strive with man always and I know their every need I assure at every promise made*

*Deep calls to calls to deep"*

Worship is one of the most powerful tools that opens the portals of heavens on the behalf of the believer. If I can make a point about worship, it helps determine your victory. There are times when in battle God will instruct you to sing your way out, to praise your way out, or simply tell Him how good He is in the midst of trouble. This action deepens your love relationship with the Father and gives the assurance that He is with us no matter what awaits us. No matter of the battle or what type of battle, God allows it to birth a new song upon your lips. He gave Judah a new song and they sang, *"Praise the Lord; for His mercy endures forever"* – 2 Chronicles 20:21. He gave Miriam, Moses' sister a new song to sing as the children of Israel was delivered from the hand of the Egyptians - Exodus 15:1-21. She led the women into worship for God's mighty acts and excellent greatness. Hallelujah!

Oh, and let's not forget David who always gave God praise for all the mighty deliverances he received. In Psalm 32: 7, King David sings of the awesome protection and songs of victory. The song goes like this, *"For you are my hiding place; you protect me from trouble. You surround me with songs of victory. Selah"*

God gives new songs as you go into battle, while in battle, and after he has brought you out victoriously from a battle. With every new song given springs forth a new testimony of newness of Life.

### *Victory in Glory!!*

# ABOUT THE AUTHOR

*Prophetess Kim Sharpton is an articulate, extraordinary and profound apostolic-prophetic voice in the nation.*

Called from her mother's womb to proclaim the gospel with such demonstration of power and signs and wonders which follow. She is mantled with humility and anointed with integrity. Her awesome prophetic intercession prayer ministry, and unique style is to bring healing and deliverance to captives to guide them into transformative living and victory. Pastor Kim Sharpton declares in the times of trouble, that Jesus gives victory and makes all things new.

As she continues to maintain values and standards of an honorable woman, she's not only a role model for women around the world in international forums, but also for her family and friends.

Prophetess Sharpton studied Behavior Health /Human services with an emphasis on counseling at Community College of Philadelphia where she earned her associate degree and two certificates - one in Human Services and one in Addiction Studies (2010). She continued to pursue her education at Chestnut Hill College and earned her Bachelor of Arts degree in Human Services (2013). She is now pursuing her Master of Art Degree in Christian Studies, with an emphasis on Pastoral Ministry at Grand Canyon University(2018).

Prophetess Sharpton has been featured on the telecast called "Ordinary People and Extraordinary God." She also has had two Internet radio broadcasts, one called "Life Solutions" on *Fmhdms radio.com* and the other called "Words of Life" which aired on *BigBadRadio.com*.

Prophetess Sharpton utilizes her capabilities in the teaching field, pastoring, preaching and teaching the Gospel of Jesus Christ. She trains in the levels of intercessory prayer and spiritual warfare in local spectrums; teaching leaders the importance of being mantled to pray and do spiritual warfare. This helps them to be able to help their congregation gain victory and walk in the newness of life. She is an author, and the Pastor and Overseer of Nikao Life Ministries and Kim Sharpton Ministries - a global, apostolic and prophetic, itinerant ministry for the saving of souls. Her life-changing messages have transformed lives all around the world.

Prophetess Kim Sharpton is the daughter of Mary C. Sharpton; the mother of three children, two daughters and one son; and the grandmother of ten grandchildren.

Using the Word of God as a guide, author-prophetess Kim continues to minister to women of all walks of life to establish the holistic design that will cause them to go after God with their whole heart, mind and soul. This will enable them to be all that God intended them to be.

# RETRIEVAL ABSTRACTION

Chapter 1
Definition Victorious - Strong's Greek 3534 nikoas

Definition afflictions –thlibo Vine's Greek New Testament Dictionary

Definition overcome -www.merriam-webster.com/dictionary/**overcome**
www.merriam-webster.com/dictionary/**steal**

Definition Jealous –zelos-Strong's Greek 2205

Joseph a type of Christ -
www.biblecharts.org/oldtestament/josephatypeofchrist.pdf


Chapter 2

It is God's divine order to protect and guide you until you give birth to vision
Definition Grace in two-fold meaning –www.bible dictionary .com


Chapter 3
Grace is designed to be Tailor made for your life
Definition Lie Pseudo –www.dictionary.com


Chapter 4
Overcome mental bondage and walk in mental freedom
Definition Mental bondage
www.studymode.com
Definition of fear –www.dictionary.com
https://www.psychologytoday.com/.../**emotional-freed**...

Chapter 5
Don't stop dreaming
Definition of dreams – 415 Dream- The prophet dictionary pg. 181
416 Dream Angel -The Prophet Dictionary pg. 182
www.joycemeyer.org/articles/ea.aspx?.a_sound_mind


Chapter 6

The purpose of Oneness


Chapter 7

Delivered - by the power of praise

Fred Hammond –when the spirit of the Lord falls upon my heart /Fred Hammond lyrics www.metro lyrics
167.50 my price for freedom /Kim Sharpton


Chapter 8

Victim to victor
WWW.Bible .org /story of Ruth and Boaz
www.bible.org/story of Adam and Eve


Chapter 9

Wisdom win
Dr. Creflo Dollar /Winning in trouble times
Strong's Hebrew: 7812. שָׁחָה (shachah) -- to bow down
Webster definition of worship

Strong's Greek: 5479. χαρά (chara) -- joy, delight - Bible
*biblehub.com/greek/5479.htm*
www.dictionary.com/browse/**patience**
www.gotquestions.org/**fruit**-**H**oly-**S**pirit-**patience**.html

**Chapter 10**
**Let nothing separate you from Loving one another**
www.merriam-webster.com/dictionary/**control**

**Chapter 11**

**The dynamics of negative words**

**Administration for children and families**
**Protecting children & strengthening families**
dictionary.reverso.net/english-cobuild/**lame%20excuse**

**Chapter 12**

**Comfort and console**

**Chapter 13**

**She's a jewel**

**Chapter 14**

**Dynamics of Love**

## Chapter 15

**Victoriously – He makes all things new**

**Seasons /Winter /Summer/Autumn /Spring**
www.**encyclopedia**.com/topic/**seasons**.aspx
 Donald Lawrence /Lyrics seasons
www.azlyrics.com/lyrics/**donaldlawrence/seasons**.html
Anita Baker Lyrics
www.az**lyrics**.com/**lyrics**/**anitabaker**/youbringme**joy**.html


## Chapter 16

Deep Calls to Deep is my personal song it's copy written already under Kim's songs inspirational songs

2 Chronicles 20:21 -www.Biblegateway.com

Exodus 15: 1-21 Song of Miriam
overview bible/bible songs

Psalm 32:7 -David's song of protection
www.Biblegateway.com